How Your Child Thinks

How Your Child Thinks

Give Your Child the Superpowers to Be a Happy, Healthy Person

DR. STEPHEN BRIERS

Vice President, Publisher: Tim Moore
Associate Publisher and Director of Marketing: Amy Neidlinger
Acquisitions Editor: Jennifer Simon
Editorial Assistant: Pamela Boland
Development Editor: Russ Hall
Operations Manager: Gina Kanouse
Digital Marketing Manager: Julie Phifer
Publicity Manager: Laura Czaja
Assistant Marketing Manager: Megan Colvin
Cover Designer: Alan Clements
Managing Editor: Kristy Hart
Senior Project Editor: Lori Lyons
Copy Editor: Krista Hansing Editorial Services
Proofreader: Water Crest Publishing
Senior Indexer: Cheryl Lenser
Interior Designer/Compositor: Gloria Schurick
Manufacturing Buyer: Dan Uhrig

©2009 by Pearson Education, Inc.
Publishing as FT Press
Upper Saddle River, New Jersey 07458

FT Press offers excellent discounts on this book when ordered in quantity for bulk purchases or special sales. For more information, please contact U.S. Corporate and Government Sales, 1-800-382-3419, corpsales@pearsontechgroup.com. For sales outside the U.S., please contact International Sales at international@pearson.com.

Company and product names mentioned herein are the trademarks or registered trademarks of their respective owners.

Printed in the United States of America
First Printing February 2009

ISBN-10: 0-13-815674-3
ISBN-13: 978-0-13-815674-9

Pearson Education LTD.
Pearson Education Australia PTY, Limited.
Pearson Education Singapore, Pte. Ltd.
Pearson Education North Asia, Ltd.
Pearson Education Canada, Ltd.
Pearson Educación de Mexico, S.A. de C.V.
Pearson Education—Japan
Pearson Education Malaysia, Pte. Ltd.

Library of Congress Cataloging-in-Publication Data

Briers, Stephen, 1965-
    How your child thinks : give your child the super powers to be a happy, healthy person / Stephen Briers.
        p. cm.
    Includes bibliographical references and index.
    ISBN 0-13-815674-3 (pbk. : alk. paper) 1. Child development. 2. Child psychology. 3. Child rearing.
I. Title.
    HQ772.B78 2009
    155.4'182—dc22
                                            2008036435

For my family.

Contents

Contents

Acknowledgments

Grateful thanks to my colleagues John McKeown and Dr. Kate Alexander for their support and insightful comments during the writing of this book. Special thanks to my very dear wife, Mel, who always underestimates her own superpowers, but has come to my rescue more times than I can count. Finally, I want to thank my boys, Joe and Will, for making me proud to be their father and helping me want to become a better one. And yes, Joe, I really *am* a psychologist...

About the Author

Before training as a clinical psychologist, Stephen studied at Cambridge University where he was later employed in child development research at the Winnicott Unit. Today Stephen works clinically with both children and adults. His various television appearances include four series of the popular BBC parenting programs *Little Angels*, *Teen Angels*, and *Make Me a Grown-Up*. He lives and works in Brighton with his wife and two young sons.

Introduction

Parenting is not easy. However much we love our children, and however much joy they bring, sometimes they push us to our limits. We are left feeling emotionally, mentally, and physically drained. At such moments, what parent *wouldn't* wish for superpowers? How fantastic it would be if we could instantly transform our children's behavior, make them see reason, or magically erase their troubles.

Unfortunately, even this book can't make it quite that easy. There are no magic wands, no quick-fix solutions, no one-size-fits-all answers. However, before you rush off to the bookseller to demand your refund, consider this: Perhaps we parents are not the ones most in need of such super-powers. What difference would it make to our children's lives (and ours) if they were more capable of managing themselves in the very situations that end up running us ragged?

This book is designed to help parents equip children to cope better with life. You may not be able to bestow super-human powers on your offspring, but you certainly can teach skills, tactics, and strategies that will significantly increase your child's own capacity for self-control. I know from experience that if children learn to apply such tools consistently, the results can be dramatic.

Training children to develop these "superpowers" is most effective when done daily, and parents can introduce these

1

tactics when children are still very young. It's important to stress that this is a proactive way of parenting, not a reactive one. Instead of waiting for bad behavior to surface and then having to deal with it, we can teach our children skills that will help reduce the likelihood of that bad behavior ever happening in the first place. And, rather magically, these same skills and abilities will help children feel happier, less pressured by life, and more able to deal with their own feelings, other people, and the world around them.

These superpowers don't have to be taught in a formal sense. In fact, they are best introduced gently, without drawing attention to them, as part of daily life. The aim of this book is to provide you with the ideas and the know-how so that when tricky situations crop up or you sense a storm brewing, you are already prepared and primed with all the strategies and skills you need to deal deftly with the situation.

The Rise of the Guilty Parent

Previous generations of parents would probably shake their heads in wonder at the idea of us all striving to be better parents. In the old days, childrearing was just common sense or a traditional way of doing things, handed down largely unquestioned from one generation to the next. Parents were simply parents; it was their children who were more likely to be labeled "good" or "bad." All that has changed. Since the 1960s, it has become almost heretical to suggest that a child might be held personally responsible for undesirable behavior.

The explanation for this shift lies with the behaviorists, founded by psychologist B. F. Skinner. Between the 1930s and 1950s, the behaviorists built on the work of Pavlov (of drooling dog fame) and promoted the extreme position that all human behavior can be reduced to a chain of cause and effect. Behind the smokescreen of the liberal, free-thinking 1960s, these behaviorist assumptions were infil-trating every aspect of our thinking—and nowhere more strongly than in our beliefs about parenting.

The end result is that we now see the badly behaved child as the victim of an inadequate or flawed upbringing. If *only* the parents had been more consistent…. If *only* they had set and maintained boundaries…. Handled differently, it surely stands to reason that little Laura would now be a model cit-izen, not the obnoxious delinquent she has become. Although there may be some truth in this, there is a real danger that such a simplistic view does little justice to either Laura or her parents. This kind of approach encour-ages us to think of children as biological machines to be programmed rather than sentient human beings strug-gling to make sense of themselves and their environment.

However, the outcome is that our parenting, like so many aspects of modern life, is now subject to constant scrutiny and evaluation from both within and without. Never has parenting been such a self-conscious and guilt-stricken affair. We strive to do the best we can, and when our chil-dren do misbehave, we feel that we have little choice but to point the finger squarely back at ourselves.

Everything from public displays of antisocial behavior to TV programs play into such anxieties and often reinforce a behavioral analysis of the problem. Bad parenting is always to blame. The media (and, as a contributor to various public television parenting series, I must put my hands up here) offers endless advice on "fixing" problem behavior using practical behavioral techniques ranging from star charts to naughty steps. The continuing popularity of such TV programs testifies to the sincere desire of parents to do their best for their children, the universality of the struggle with defiant and difficult behavior, and the underlying insecurity that sometimes leads us to compare ourselves with other moms and dads. We all want to get it right.

Although the techniques shown on such programs are genuinely helpful, they sometimes create the misleading impression that star charts and naughty steps are the solution to all our children's problems.

Moving Beyond the "Carrot and Stick" Approach

I want to make it clear that I am by no means opposed to behaviorist approaches, *per se*. Such techniques have been tremendously empowering for many parents and provided them with effective strategies for calming troubled waters. Children undoubtedly *do* respond well to suitable boundaries, and the judicious administration of carrot-and-stick plays an important role in good parenting. In my clinics, I regularly recommend such approaches as an important aspect of supporting a child's development and emotional adjustment.

But this is precisely my point: However important they are, conditioning techniques represent only *one* aspect of the bigger picture. Our society is in increasing danger of mistaking the part for the whole and developing a fixation on the symptom rather than the cause. Is the highest accolade of our parenting really the eradication of "problem behavior"? Are we losing sight of the important truth behind Jess Lear's astute (if slightly oversweet) observation that "Children are not things to be molded, but are people to be unfolded?"

A shift in the parenting agenda is long overdue. We need to move the focus away from containing problem behavior after it surfaces and pay more attention to developing the psychological skills children need to manage their lives. Prevention really *is* better than cure, and if we can equip children with the relevant skills, they stand a good chance of heading off not only their own bad behavior, but also a host of potential mental health problems before they take root.

Protecting Your Child's Mind

As parents, we need to be thinking about how we can protect the mental health of the next generation. Surveys and statistics are released almost weekly indicating that mental illness of all kinds is on the increase and that young people may be especially vulnerable. Evidence suggests that there are more depressed children in our midst than ever before and that the average onset of the emotional disorders is happening earlier.

In the United States, Professor Martin Seligman's rigorous analysis of four large-scale American studies across different age groups leads him to an alarming conclusion: Since the 1950s, there has been "more depression, beginning younger and younger." Seligman refers to an "epidemic of depression" and points out how crucial it is that preventative steps are taken to counter its debilitating impact among young people.

In view of such figures, it seems clear that modern parents *must* now be thinking beyond merely controlling bad behavior, especially because (particularly in the case of boys) acting-up behavior itself could be symptomatic of an underlying emotional disturbance.

Seligman and colleagues found that by cultivating specific habits of thought using simple cognitive behavioral techniques, it is possible to provide children with a level of psychological inoculation against depressive illness. These techniques are simple to teach and have been carefully assessed to establish their effectiveness. There's no reason why we parents shouldn't teach our children these skills to help safeguard their mental health, in the same way that we teach them how to brush their teeth to keep them from getting tooth decay.

Of course, the value of teaching psychological life skills to kids is not just about preventing things from going wrong— it's about giving children tools that can enhance their sense of competence, self-esteem, and fulfillment. Over the past few decades, the Positive Psychology movement has produced some revealing insights into what makes people happy and emotionally well balanced. We now have a much better idea of what skills and mindsets promote happiness and well-being, and we know that these skills and mindsets can be learned. This book shows you how to help your children develop them.

What Does "Discipline" Really Mean?

A common view holds that children of the PlayStation generation are less well disciplined than their predecessors. However, we tend to ignore the fact that the word *discipline* has several meanings. It's now generally associated with correction and punishment, but the original Latin root of the word *disciplina* implies a mentoring relationship: The pupil or "disciple" submits to instruction to hone his skills and realize his potential. This is an aspect of discipline we are at risk of neglecting in modern parenting.

Having worked clinically with children, my conviction is that if we can teach our children how to recognize and manage their own thoughts and feelings at a much earlier age, the "problem behavior" that preoccupies our current concept of childrearing might actually become less of a problem for all of us. If we invest in equipping them with the mental tools they need, our children will become less reliant on bad behavior and will find more productive ways to resolve their problems.

Already I can hear you thinking to yourself, "This sounds all very well in theory, but has he forgotten that we are talking about *children* here? Don't the skills he's referring to require a level of sophistication well beyond the scope of most youngsters?" Fortunately, the answer on both counts is "No."

In the first place, despite what professional clinicians might have you believe, much of the more practical end of psychology is hardly rocket science. Clinicians routinely teach many of these techniques to children in their consulting rooms. Sadly, however, the children concerned are not usually equipped with these skills until things have become bad enough for their parents or teachers to seek professional help.

With a little creativity, we can teach these skills in different ways at different levels of complexity, according to the age and capacity of each child. One of the aims of this book is to demonstrate how the techniques described can be adapted to make them relevant even to very young children. To maximize the protective and life-enhancing benefits of these skills, ideally, we should lay the foundation at a much earlier age than you might assume possible. Although practical experience suggests that even young children can master these techniques, new research findings also suggest that children are far more competent and capable than we have previously been led to believe.

Your Amazing Child

Perhaps one of the most damaging legacies of behaviorism has been the subjective vision it has given us of children themselves. Although the discipline of psychology has happily moved on, the sad reality is that, in parenting circles, we continue to treat children like little "black boxes." Their internal workings are allowed to remain a mystery while we both discredit and underestimate their intelligence. We tend to see children not as young minds striving to make sense of their world, but as bundles of impulses, appetites, and reflexes that, in Lear's words, must be "molded" toward social conformity.

Unfortunately, it is not just behaviorism that has biased our conception of childhood—ironically, it's joined by a branch of developmental psychology that at first glance seems to offer an antidote to the limitations of the behaviorist approach. Unlike many psychologists of his day, Jean Piaget was deeply interested in the child's mental world. His great contribution was a vision of a child's intelligence expanding progressively through a succession of stages, each representing an extension and refinement of the stage before.

The field of child development owes a great debt to Piaget—he made huge contributions to our understanding. Unfortunately, however, his stages of development are tied fairly rigidly to ages and has led us to make assumptions about what children are capable of understanding and when. The trouble is that such expectations tend to become self-fulfilling: If we assume that a younger child cannot hope to grasp a concept, we make no effort to teach it; because we do not teach it, the child never demonstrates the skill and, thus, reinforces our belief that he is incapable of learning it.

9

The exciting twist in the story is that the latest experimental research suggests that even very young infants have far greater intellectual powers than was ever assumed possible. Meanwhile, new findings in the field of neuroscience bring us closer to understanding how to unlock this potential.

For example, it now appears that infants as young as three to four months have the beginnings of a working knowledge of the physical world. They know that an object will fall if not supported and that a ball requires a push to set it in motion. Children as young as five months can actually count up to three.

More relevant for the purposes of this book, young children also appear to have much greater capacity for abstract thinking than the theories of Piaget allow. They are able to "learn about learning" even from a very young age. Experimental evidence shows that they can stand back and evaluate strategies used for solving problems, whereas previously it was assumed that they lacked the reflective abilities required to do this. Children don't simply rely on trial and error, repeatedly forcing the square peg into the round hole until it works. New findings suggest that, in certain circumstances, children are capable of much higher-level thinking than we formerly thought possible.

Many of the skills described in this book are geared toward helping children solve emotional and thinking problems. They require children to become aware of their own internal processes and to figure out what works and what doesn't when they encounter difficulties in their mental and social worlds. Although clinical experience suggests that most children are more than up to the task when given appropriate support, it is reassuring that the research evidence confirms that these abilities lie comfortably within their grasp.

$$E = mc^2$$

Too Much Like Hard Work?

Even if it is technically possible for children to master such skills, doesn't it drain some of the fun and spontaneity out of childhood? Isn't it all a bit serious? Shouldn't we let our children just enjoy being kids?

I entirely agree that it is vital to give children the space and freedom to enjoy and discover themselves through unstructured play. We are right to distrust the kind of hot-housing of children that so often stems from insecurity or the invidious desire to compare children's accomplishments with those of neighbors or friends. Jokes about flashcards in the womb are sometimes a little close to home, and is there really any long-term advantage if my child learns to read a year ahead of her best friend?

However, to suggest that we shouldn't try to help improve our children's self-control and give them key psychological skills on the grounds that it takes the fun out of childhood suggests a misunderstanding of the kinds of skills we're talking about and perhaps a somewhat rose-tinted vision of what it's actually like to be a child.

Whether they are aware of it or not, parents teach their children all the time. Not only do children learn by observing us and following our example, but parents already help their children structure problems or contain their anxieties and fears as a matter of course.

Parents can use the techniques described in this book in this kind of daily real-life situation. This shouldn't feel like hard work: Parents can weave this training quite naturally into everyday living, at times when you'd normally be thinking about what to say to your child or how to help her deal with what's happening. The tools and strategies will hopefully come alive for your child because you can introduce them within the context of practical, real-life situations as needed.

Isn't it better to lay a careful foundation of "right thinking" from the outset rather than have to undo destructive patterns later? Good or bad, such habits take many years to consolidate, and anyone who has tried to break a habit of any kind already knows how difficult that can be. Isn't it worth investing in a bit of informal mental coaching with your child to ensure that such bad habits never get a stranglehold in the first place?

We also need to bear in mind how easy it is for us to entertain romantic notions of what it's like to be a child. Contrary to popular belief, very few of us experience childhood as a carefree Elysium of endless summers and sweet, dreamless nights.

Just think about it for a moment: As a child, you are physically and intellectually punier than the adults all around you and utterly dependent upon them for your bodily and emotional survival. You have precious little control over your life. All the big decisions and many of the minor ones are made for you. As a rule, you are expected to do what you're told, regardless of what you might want. Frustratingly, you often don't even know what you *do* want. The world around you might be full of wonder, but it also reveals itself to be a place of unfathomable terrors. Unfortunately for you, you lack the experience to know which is which. The more you learn, the more alarming it can all seem. To top it off, your body keeps changing size and shape at an unpredictable rate, and you find yourself at the mercy of powerful waves of emotion that can completely overwhelm you at a moment's notice.

Not sounding so appealing now? The whole point about improving your children's capacity for self-regulation is that you are helping empower one of the world's most disenfranchised populations. Instead of stripping the magic out of childhood, chances are that with these skills under their belt, children will actually be in a better position to enjoy a more carefree and happy childhood—and hopefully a more carefree and happy adulthood.

Teaching children psychological life skills from an early age is not only possible, but it also represents a sound investment in your child's happiness and mental well-being. Research suggests that children are equipped to learn, so now it's up to us as parents to equip ourselves to teach.

This book is designed to do just that—to introduce you to tools and concepts you should find useful in the quest to be a better parent. In applying them, hopefully we can all move a little further away from the naughty step.

It is time to expand our definition of "good parenting." We need a more proactive vision in which we take responsibility for equipping the next generation with the life skills they need to cope with the stresses of modern living. To do so effectively, we must teach our children how to master both the challenges of the world around them and the equally demanding terrain of their own minds.

Author's Note

A few words about the way the book is written.... Although you will find some examples involving children I have met in my clinical work, naturally I have changed names and certain details to protect their anonymity. Occasionally I have featured cases that are a compilation of several real children because this turned out to be the best way to draw out the relevant points.

Grammatically, I have used the pronouns *he* and *she* interchangeably throughout the text. This isn't just about political correctness: It's very hard to do anything else. Please mentally translate this into the language that relates to the gender of your own children.

Chapters 2–7 each contain one central topic and a cluster of related skills. However, as you will see, there are many themes that run throughout the book, and a number of the techniques described can be applied to a range of different contexts. Please feel free to think flexibly about how you can make the content most relevant to your child's life.

Most of the specific techniques I described in the book are taken from standard clinical practice. These are the sorts of things you and your child would learn from a child clinical psychologist in a professional capacity. I can take personal credit for very few of the ideas in this book—what I hope I have done is present the current research and state-of-the-art clinical strategies in a clear and accessible form that helps you, as a parent, to begin applying these techniques as part of your childrearing.

If you do find yourself struggling, I encourage you not to give up—instead, consult someone who might be able to help you become proficient with these tools. You can find a lot of helpful guides out there, and I have included suggestions for further reading, in case you feel you need more support or information.

Finally, I hope that reading this book is an enjoyable experience for you. The minds of children offer a fascinating world to explore, and I hope you will find information in the pages that follow that will inspire as well as inform.

ONE

X-Ray Vision:
What's Going On Inside?

Psychologists are trained to notice not only what their clients say and do, but also how their clients make them feel. This is called "counter-transference" and can provide vital clues about the client's inner world. For example, if I find myself feeling inexplicably downcast before a certain client's sessions, this might tell me something about that client's own state of mind.

So what happens if we apply this principle of counter-transference to our encounters with misbehaving children? What do we typically feel as parents at such moments? And what can that tell us about how our children are feeling?

Speaking personally, the first thing I usually experience is a surge of internal pressure that, unless I am careful, prompts me to explode right back in their faces. The strength of feeling that even quite mild child misbehavior can evoke is surprising. Whatever control I muster on the surface, I am conscious of an inner voice screaming that it has got to STOP before the internal pressure becomes unbearable. Quite irrationally, I can experience my kids' conduct as a violation of my boundaries, as an intrusion or an attack. I can even feel that things are starting to fall apart, literally disintegrating around me. At another level, I also feel embarrassed, ashamed that their conduct has deviated so far from what it should be, from what *I* want it to be.

Every parent knows that the company of a screaming toddler can be a bizarrely humiliating experience. In my consulting rooms, many parents confess that they have never felt as helpless as when they are unable to manage their children's behavior. I suspect it is the unique power of our children to confront us at such times with our own buried vulnerabilities that can make parental discipline such an emotive issue for us all.

In the face of such uncomfortable feelings, the natural priority is to strike back and attempt to halt the disturbing behavior as swiftly as possible. Dismissing a child as "bad" under these circumstances is one tempting means of sealing off such distressing emotions and disconnecting ourselves from the source. However, although at such times we might want to distance ourselves emotionally from our children, it is important to consider our own reactions as a useful window into what it is like for the child in the throes of the tantrum.

If we scratch the surface of a badly behaved child's defiance, we'll probably find something not far removed from the adult's experience: a soul in some degree of torment, battling with a succession of gut-wrenching emotions—someone who feels helpless, ashamed, and ultimately humiliated by his or her own lack of control.

In a fantastic chapter in P. L. Travers's *Mary Poppins*, called "Bad Tuesday," Michael Banks wakes up with "a curious feeling" inside him. Under the irresistible influence of this strange mood, Michael diagnoses (quite correctly) that he is going to be naughty. And he certainly is. He is insolent to the housemaid, the cook, his mother, and even—most thrillingly—to the formidable Mary Poppins herself.

Uncharacteristically, Mary Poppins largely ignores Michael's provocative behavior. With the aid of a mysterious compass, she soon whisks the children to the four corners of the globe, where they encounter, respectively, a polar bear, a hyacinth macaw, a panda, and a dolphin. The various animals give the children a warm and friendly welcome. However, even the distraction of this magical mystery tour has little effect on Michael's glowering mood and deteriorating conduct. Eventually, he steals the compass and attempts to escape from his family. But unfortunately for Michael, Mary Poppins's grim prophecy that Master Banks has "got something coming to him" proves alarmingly accurate. Michael unwittingly summons up a nightmarish vision of the four animals, this time incarnated as feral, vicious predators who bear down menacingly upon him from the four corners of the room. Michael drops the compass in terror and screams out for Mary Poppins. Predictably, she arrives on cue and order is smoothly restored.

Now, a straightforward reading is that this is a tale of a willful child who gets his just deserts. In what for the parental reader is a satisfying twist, Michael brings upon himself due retribution for his bad behavior. However, what is so interesting about this chapter is the commentary it provides on the experience of such "naughtiness" from the child's perspective.

What seems clear is that Michael is at the mercy of internal forces he cannot really control. While he may put up little resistance, the strange feeling with which he awakes effectively drives him from one act of naughtiness to the next with an inevitable momentum. At various points, he attempts to "own" his deviance, resisting all attempts to make him feel apologetic and driving his bad behavior forward, but the reality seems to be that, in this state, Michael has limited jurisdiction over his actions.

It is significant that the book's heroine, that reliable champion of decorum, good manners, and an impeccable appearance, makes so little attempt to rebuke him. Mary Poppins treats Michael as if he is in a state of diminished responsibility.

Certainly, as matters deteriorate, Michael seems to find himself cut adrift from familiar sources of support, both internal and external. He becomes unable to relate to the people or perspectives that might anchor him. Even Mary Poppins's reproach has little effect upon him. Eventually, Michael is reduced to a state of utter powerlessness and becomes easy prey for the terrifying phantasms he has unleashed.

The story is compelling for children, not least because they recognize the fundamental truth of Michael's plight: However deliberate it may look, to be caught up in the extremes of "bad behavior" involves a loss of self-control and is an experience that ushers in elements of genuine fear and disorientation. Michael might not put up a particularly good fight, but P. L. Travers portrays him as much victim as perpetrator.

> Bad behavior involves a loss of self-control, and that can be a frightening and unpleasant experience for the child as well as the parent.

Closer to Home

I remember an incident when, for some reason I cannot recall now, my ten-year-old son erupted in anger and started swearing at me in front of his grandparents, who were visiting at the time. I was shocked by the language, outraged by my son's rudeness, and mortified that this unsavory episode was playing out in front of my wife's parents, who (according to family lore) had magically conjured the highest standards of behavior from their own three children. With a certain satisfaction, I readied myself for the blast of frosty disapproval that my son was about to unleash from his grandparents.

Imagine my surprise when, instead, his grandmother's eyes filled with tears and she started pleading with me to "help him." Now, at this juncture, the only "help" I was picturing myself offering my son was being administered, Homer Simpson style, with both hands firmly around his neck. However, what my mother-in-law recognized was something that the heat of my own indignation had hidden from me: that being as wound up as my son had become is actually a very threatening mental space to inhabit. As she explained to me later, "I know what it's like to get into that place where you just can't get back again...."

I am not implying that all children's bad behavior should simply be excused or dismissed because of how upsetting it can be for them. On the contrary, a cornerstone of the approach in this book is that children should be encouraged to take *more* responsibility for their behavior, not less. However, if we expect children to master their antisocial impulses, we also need to give them the skills and techniques to do so.

All too often in the way we deal with children's tantrums or outbursts, we talk to them as if they were simply electing to be defiant or difficult, and that it would be just as easy for them to switch off their bad behavior and simply choose to be "good." The reality is that even as adults, we do not always find this easy—but for children, impulse control is an especially demanding task.

> If we want our children to master antisocial impulses, we must give them the skills to be able to do it.
>
>

Why Is It So Hard for Children to Control Themselves?

Self-control is not traditionally part of a child's job description, but over the last 20 years, scientists have gathered a lot more information about why children are particularly prone to failures of self-control, compared with adults.

Let me introduce Ben. Ben tends to do whatever comes into his head, apparently without pausing to think about the impact or consequences of his actions. Emotionally unpredictable, Ben's behavior is often atrocious—so bad, in fact, that going out with him in public can be a nightmare. Ben couldn't care less. His family says that he seems to have no "off" button. His manners are nonexistent, he has the attention span of a gnat, and his reckless, confrontational behavior means he is constantly getting himself into trouble. Ben displays a total disregard for rules and regulations, and often comes across as selfish, boastful, and immature.

Ben cuts an unattractive figure. We have all come across children who behave like Ben and, if we are honest, at times we can recognize elements of Ben in even the most immaculately behaved child. Ben, however, is not a child. He is a 45-year-old adult and, prior to a car accident eight months ago, his personality and behavior were very different. He was a gentle, shy, cultivated man, much loved by his friends and respected by his work colleagues. Ben suffers from a condition called orbitofrontal syndrome, a pattern of disinhibited emotion and behavior caused by damage to a particular part of his brain.

Cases of brain injury such as Ben's have given researchers invaluable insights into how the brain works and have been enormously helpful in mapping how different areas of the brain relate to specific abilities. Interestingly, neuroscientists have also discovered that the area of the brain damaged in Ben's case does not fully develop in perfectly normal human beings until well into their teenage years.

In the language of cognitive psychology, the prefrontal cortex is the command center for the "cool system." This is the counterpart of—you guessed it—the "hot system." It seems that our ability to exercise effective self-control depends upon the way these two systems interact.

The hot system is designed to produce rapid, automatic reactions to aspects of the environment that we need to be attracted to or repelled by. The hot system fires up almost instantaneously and dominates in situations where we find ourselves acting on the spur of the moment or responding to gut instinct. Sometimes called the "emotional" brain, the hot system drives the sort of primal instincts that helped our ancestors find food and mates and avoid predators. It can rapidly create powerful states of arousal that encourage us to approach or avoid relevant hot-spot stimuli. Physically, the control center for the hot system seems to be located in the amygdala, a small almond-shaped area in the primitive forebrain.

By contrast, the cool system gives us our ability to process more complex aspects of the world. The cool system is rational, logical, and trades in the currency of information instead of high-octane emotion. With help from the intricate switchboard of the hippocampus and the frontal lobes, the cool system enables us to reflect on experience, analyze it, and generate new strategies for moving forward.

Although functionally distinct, these two systems are linked. It is thought that neural connections wire up various hot spots and cool nodes within the brain. This web of connections gives the cool system the power to deactivate hot spots when appropriate. When temptation strikes and we fight off the urge to have a cigarette by reminding ourselves of the health risks, deliberately distracting ourselves or putting into place a contingency plan, we are using cooling strategies to dampen a hot-system stimulus.

In children, the cooling system takes time to evolve. A combination of fewer cool nodes and poor connections with relevant hot spots tends to leave children at the mercy of their hot system impulses.

Although I'm not tying to suggest that all children are brain-damaged, into the teen years, even a perfectly normal child has neurological limitations that show up on a scan. These correspond with psychological limitations with which you may be all too familiar.

During adolescence, a time when the brain overall actually prunes back millions of redundant neural pathways, the density of neural branching in the prefrontal cortex actually becomes richer and more elaborate. This is significant because of the role the prefrontal cortex plays in impulse control and decision making. One implication could be that we need to provide appropriate challenges to stimulate this process of development. However, the key point is that the prefrontal cortex of the human brain, the seat of the cooling system, is simply not fully formed until adulthood. As a result, it doesn't always work that efficiently in younger children.

So next time you're confronted with a histrionic outburst, unbearable moodiness, mad-cap risk taking, or an infantile tantrum, take a deep breath. Before you condemn yourself as a terrible parent or label your child as the spawn of Satan, spare a thought for the role played by biological time-tabling.

The rational cooling system in the brain takes time to evolve and isn't properly developed until adulthood.

A System Under Strain

When it comes to self-regulation, it's not just the neural hardware in children's brains that is overdue for an upgrade: The same is true of the software. As we grow older, more and more of what we do becomes a matter of habit. When you stop to think about it, even apparently simple tasks such as brushing your teeth involve miraculous feats of coordination and perceptual judgment. When we learn a new skill, the process of acquisition is time consuming and effortful. Anyone who doubts this has only to witness the furrowed concentration on a young child's face as he begins to form clumsy letters with a pencil, or the focus required by a toddler as she takes her first faltering steps.

In time, tasks that demand such conscious expenditure of mental energy in the early stages become automatic and effortless. The brain creates efficient protocols for walking, writing, and riding a bicycle, for example, which fortunately mean that such activities largely take care of themselves. Once learned, these tasks no longer drain the mind's resources as they did to begin with, so the mind can more freely be channeled toward other goals. Soon you can ride a bike and simultaneously think about what you want to have for dinner. Ask a preschooler what she wants for a snack during her initial outing on two wheels, though, and she'll most likely end up in the bushes.

The fact is that the brain's processing power, particularly our capacity to devote conscious attention to things, is a finite resource. As adults, we benefit from having already automated many aspects of our lives and can depend on unconscious sub-routines to deal fairly reliably with the everyday stuff (although at times we might still discover our toothbrush primed with moisturizer or find our wallet in the fridge). Children, by contrast, are still assimilating many of the skills we take for granted. This means that, on a daily basis, their concentration is being taxed to a much greater degree just by the routine business of everyday life.

The reason this is so relevant when thinking about children's misbehavior is that the regions of the brain involved in so-called "executive functions"—such as planning, solving complex problems, evaluating choices, and switching between activities—are precisely the same ones that enable us to inhibit impulses and regulate our feelings. This means that mental tasks involving a lot of processing power, even in seemingly unrelated domains, might have a cumulative effect on children's ability to keep their behavior in check. Put simply, self-control is a form of mental labor. If mental effort is being expended in other directions, there may not be enough gas left in the tank to fuel the engine of self-regulation.

Numerous times I have met parents deeply frustrated by their child's ability to behave angelically at school while their conduct at home is running them ragged. Their argument: "If he can manage to behave at school, why can't he do so at home?" There may, of course, be several explanations for this, but, ironically, one factor could be that it is precisely *because* he is behaving well at school that he is coping more poorly at home. The exercise of self-control in one context could be using up available resources in the other. Sometimes when your child comes through the front door at the end of the school day, she might already be running on empty.

Psychologist Ron Baumeister and colleagues have provided some interesting experimental evidence for the very real demands self-control places upon us. Baumeister discovered that if you encourage a group of people to resist temptation by sitting them near a plate of cookies that they are forbidden to eat, they will give up much more quickly on a later task that involves copying complex figures. This was compared both to participants who had been allowed to eat the cookies before-hand *and* a group who performed the experiment with no food present.

On the basis of his experiments, Baumeister concluded that self-control is like a muscle. Exercising it within sensible lim-its increases its power, but self-control, or "self-regulatory strength," can also be pushed to the point of fatigue, resulting in a sudden and dramatic collapse. The way our New Year's resolutions can so readily fall apart after a stressful day at work or we find ourselves drinking more than intended after "holding it together" over the summer vacation offer everyday examples of the same phenomenon.

For children, self-control is like a muscle. Exercising it makes it stronger, but too much use makes it tired.

The fact that the frontal lobes of the brain govern various, different functions that all draw from the same mental pot suggests that if we can help increase the efficiency of some of those tasks, we likely can lighten the load on the prefrontal cortex as a whole. In theory, this should make more resources available for other functions, including self-control. For example, if we help children become better at problem solving, not only do we give them tools to handle situations in ways that will create less stress for them, but we also release the capacity to deal with any internal stress they have to tolerate.

If we are to help children master themselves, we need to adopt a holistic approach that recognizes the way these different systems connect with and influence each other. One of the problems with using carrot-and-stick methods to target specific "problem" behaviors is that they are often taken out of context. We can all too easily ignore the fact that children's ability to behave well is just one outcome of mastering several distinct but interrelated mental skills.

Where Does This Leave Us?

Now, you may be reading this thinking, "Well, if there are all these legitimate biological reasons why my child struggles to control herself, maybe I have no choice but to sit tight, grit my teeth, and wait for her brain to develop."

On the contrary, the opposite is true. In the early 1970s, Walter Mischel offered a group of four-year-olds a choice: Either they could have one marshmallow right away or, if they waited until the experimenter came back into the room, they could have two. Even at four years of age, two thirds of children successfully resisted the immediate temptation of the treat in front of them. Despite their brains not being fully mature, many of these children *were* demonstrating a measure of self-control. There would seem to be absolutely no reason why we cannot nurture this potential, just like any other innate ability. After all, we don't abandon teaching children to read in preschool because they can't hope to read with the fluency they will have attained in a few years. As with literacy, the development of self-control requires sustained input, support, and stimulation.

Particularly encouraging is the fact that many of the children who managed to hold out in Mischel's experiment exhibited basic cooling strategies, such as finding distraction and talking to themselves. This raises the intriguing possibility that the children who successfully resisted temptation were not blessed with superior willpower, but simply had better tactics for handling such dilemmas. It could be argued that it is precisely during the period when their brains are still maturing that children can benefit most from being given practical strategies to compensate for their biological shortcomings.

What is most remarkable of all is how powerfully predictive the "one treat now" trial proved to be for the children who took part. Twelve to fourteen years later, when the children from the original experiment were followed up, Mischel and his colleagues found that the "resisters" were significantly outperforming the "yielders" on a whole range of different measures. Those who had been able to wait were scoring as better adjusted, academically smarter, and more resourceful. Those who had been unable to delay gratification were more introverted, had lower self-esteem, were more temperamental, and were demonstrably less able to cope under pressure.

These results underline not only how fundamentally self-control contributes to all manner of desirable skills and attributes, but also how crucial it is that we nurture this capacity during children's formative years. I know from clinical experience that cooling strategies *can* be taught—and that they do make a difference. In the pages that follow, I introduce practical ways in which you can support and promote your child's emerging self-control skills.

TWO

Developing Super-Senses:
The ABC of Feelings

It's past midnight on a dank, misty evening. You are standing on one end of what you thought was a deserted platform in an unfamiliar town waiting for a train. Because of the fog, your visibility is limited. Your infant's stroller is at your side. There is no sign of your train. Gradually you become aware of the steady fall of footsteps coming toward you. How do you react?

By now, you are almost certainly in a state of heightened alert. You probably feel uneasy. Your pupils have dilated and your senses become heightened as you scan instinctively for visual or auditory cues that might help you assess the possible threat. Automatically, your respiratory rate has increased and oxygenated blood is diverted to your muscles and brain as your body readies itself for action.

However, you're not the only one scanning for information about an uncertain situation. The infant by your side is also staring intently. But he's not peering into the gloom trying to identify the shadowy stranger. Instead, his gaze is fixed on you. He is searching for clues to his fate in the configuration of the 42 facial muscles that you use to register emotion. Depending on what he finds in your expression, your child will either relax or become increasingly agitated.

When presented with an ambiguous or unfamiliar situation, the first place most infants look for further information is in the faces of their caregivers. This process is called "referencing." Children do this instinctively because, even though they lack the ability to assess complex situations themselves, from a very young age, they have already become adept at reading the emotions on people's faces.

Audre Lord claims that "our feelings are the most genuine path to knowledge"—but for a child, they are one of the few pathways open to him. Consequently, he greatly relies upon them. Long before his powers of reason mature, it is a child's untutored feelings that shepherd him through his period of greatest vulnerability. It is his emotions that prompt him to seek food and comfort and his emotions that keep him close to the adult caregivers he relies upon. Moreover, it is the child's emotions that alert others to his needs. His sensitivity to the feelings of others also provides him with critical data about his immediate environment.

When your baby smiles back in response to your smile, she is not simply imitating your behavior. Rather, the human brain appears to be equipped with specialized hardware that enables children to tap directly into the emotions they witness around them. How is this possible? Our knowledge has been recently advanced by the discovery of clusters of specialized brain cells known as "mirror neurons."

I Feel What You Feel

Researchers have discovered that when macaque monkeys watch other monkeys grasping objects, certain regions of their brains involved in motor coordination begin firing *just as if the spectators themselves were performing the actions.* This is remarkable. In response to a scatter of visual stimuli hitting the retina, via a mind-boggling feat of translation, similar patterns of activity occurred almost instantaneously in specific brain centers within both the doer and the observer. Put simply: These mirror neurons seemed to be helping the monkeys to get inside each other's heads. In some senses, both the performer and the observer were sharing the same experience, even though only one of them was actively taking part.

From an evolutionary point of view, this is a fantastically useful development. It enables us to update existing skills and prepare for the acquisition of new ones simply by watching others. We see a professional dancer gliding across the floor, and we instantly have an intuitive sense of what the movement would feel like—even if most of us would be hard-pressed to replicate the motion with our own bodies.

Some scientists have argued that this ability of higher primates to "participate" by watching in this way has given *homo sapiens* such a leg up the evolutionary ladder. It presumably also explains why spectating, whether in sporting arenas or theaters, can engage us like it does. We don't simply watch the running back get that winning touchdown; in our heads, we are there—running hard, with adrenaline coursing through our systems, our muscles unconsciously twitching as we anticipate diving across the goal line.

Other researchers have found compelling evidence that the neural mirroring process might also support the transmission of certain emotions. It seems likely that such cells create an empathetic bridge that gives us direct access to what another person is feeling by actually re-creating aspects of the emotion inside the observer.

For example, if you look on a magnetic resonance imaging (MRI) scanner at the brain of someone experiencing the emotion of disgust, an area of the brain called the anterior insula lights up. However, if the same person just watches someone else showing an expression of disgust, the anterior insula reacts in much the same way. A resonance of disgust is re-created inside the brain of the observer. When we see an expression on someone's face, we not only recognize what that person is feeling, but we experience an echo of that feeling ourselves.

Is It Catching?

The fact that this appears to be an innate hard-wired capacity rather than just a developed skill means that children are just as susceptible to emotional priming as adults. The English language has more than 200 words to describe our different emotions, suggesting that there are many different shades and hues of emotional experience. However, there appear to be six basic emotions at the core of our emotional lives: happiness, surprise, fear, sadness, disgust, and anger. These core feelings correspond to virtually identical facial expressions throughout the world, regardless of local culture and tradition.

Studies of young babies suggest that, from a very early age, infants recognize and respond to basic emotional cues on the faces of their caregivers. The mirror neuron research implies that babies in facial recognition trials are not just imitating what they see in front of them; to at least some degree, they are experiencing firsthand the emotions with which they are presented. When we frown at our children, they feel the chill of displeasure; when we smile and laugh, we flood them with the sunlight of their own capacity for joy.

> Your children feel what you feel. They learn their response from your response. Help rehearse them in experiencing positive emotions.
>
>

We have always instinctively understood that emotions are contagious, but neuroscience is giving us new insights into how and why. This research suggests that we need to take seriously the responsibility of monitoring the emotional climate to which our children are exposed. Similar to how a persistent trickle of water carves out a channel for itself over time, whenever we display an emotion, we are most likely priming, rehearsing, and reinforcing a bias toward the same emotional responses in our children. What they see, they not only imitate—they probably learn to feel, too.

Becoming an Emotional Coach

Before we get too anxious about the negative impact that our own moods might be having on our children, it is important to recognize the very positive opportunities that this amazing human faculty also provides. Because we can use our faces, voices, and bodies to trigger them, we can introduce children to their own emotions in a relatively controlled fashion. More important, we can use our own emotional reactions to conduct young children through emotional transitions they will later need to master themselves.

Ellie is a spirited toddler who will attend her friend Maisie's birthday party later in the afternoon. Throughout the morning, Ellie has been working herself into a state of manic excitement. She is currently discharging her mounting internal pressure by dancing around the living room and jumping off the furniture. Predictably, the only consequence of this behavior is to further escalate her levels of excitement and arousal.

Because the mirroring process works both ways, her mother, Jenny, is now also experiencing a corresponding level of agitation (and not just because she can't face the prospect of washing the sofa cushions). Under such circumstances, Jenny would, of course, be forgiven for seeking to relieve her own tension by "losing her cool" and yelling at her daughter.

However, instructing a child to "calm down" while you remain in a state of high arousal yourself sends the child a confusing double message. The words demand one response, but if Jenny pursues this strategy, the cues from her agitated body language will likely produce the opposite effect in her daughter, maintaining Ellie's rocketing arousal levels. To evoke a calmer mood in Ellie, Jenny needs to transmit behavior cues that will elicit the desired mood. This means that Jenny must either a) convincingly disguise what she is really feeling, or b) remove herself from the situation until she can get into a more relaxed state herself before tackling her daughter.

Show the change you want to see in your child. It's pointless to tell a child to calm down if you are agitated yourself. You need to calm down first so your child can see how.

Ellie needs help because she is little; as yet she lacks the capacity to regulate her own reserves of nervous energy. But her mother can give her the experience of "calming down" through exposure to adult behavioral cues aimed at inducing a calmer state of mind. Ellie will automatically pick up on her mother's nonverbal triggers through the mirroring process, so she should feel her own tension begin to dissipate.

When dealing with children's behavior, research underlines that our nonverbal communications matter just as much as the content of what we are saying. If Jenny is successful, then Ellie will at least start to get a sense of what the transition out of a highly aroused state feels like. She may not be able to replicate it on her own yet, but at least she will have another example in her repertoire to draw upon when she needs to make such a shift on her own.

If we want children to learn to regulate their own emotions, it is important that there is consistency between the emotions we describe in words and the nonverbal cues we attach to those descriptions. Otherwise, we can be talking about one feeling while unconsciously generating something very different in our children. This weakens the associations between the labels we provide and the feeling states we are trying to map onto them. Because the strength of these associations is crucial to giving the rational, thinking brain priority over the primitive feeling brain, this really does matter. When our words and our feelings become dislocated from one another, we leave ourselves at the mercy of our emotions.

Make sure your words match your body language and behavior. If you say "calm," you need to show "calm."

Learning to Label Emotions

To be able to regulate their emotions, children first need to know what they *are* feeling. They must also be able to separate themselves from the experience of feeling so they can see what's happening to them. This is the difference between allowing yourself to be carried along in the current of a powerful river and finding a secure position on the bank from which to observe the seething waters in front of you. To process experience, the thinking brain needs to translate it into terms that it can deal with.

In most undergraduate psychology courses, students learn that the Inuit people have many different words for types of snow, whereas in English we have only one. The example illustrates the interrelationship between thought, perception, and language.

The idea is that because the Inuit people have more snow-related vocabulary, they also experience whole dimensions of snow that we Westerners are unaware of—our poverty of words and concepts in this area restricts what we can see. To us, snow is just snow. Our lack of language leaves us unattuned to the more subtle distinctions that an Eskimo might discern between *aput* ("snow on the ground") and *piqsirpoq* ("drifting snow"). Unlike our Inuit cousins, we are partially "snow-blind."

This is the basis of the imposingly entitled "Sapir-Whorf linguistic hypothesis": What we *can* think depends upon the availability of the appropriate words to help us think it. Ironically, it turns out that the Inuit snow vocabulary has been somewhat overplayed. By 1978, the seven words for *snow* that Benjamin Whorf mentions in his 1940s article had mysteriously reached 50, thanks to the exaggeration of later writers. By 1984, *The New York Times* was referring to a hundred different terms.

Although this famous example no longer packs quite the same punch, and linguists and philosophers now question whether vocabulary alone determines what we can think, a valid principle remains at the heart of Sapir and Whorf's theory: Our children do require a reliable emotional vocabulary if they are to make meaningful distinctions between feeling states and develop workable strategies to manage them.

> Children need to learn words for what they are feeling.
>
>

It is striking that in our culture the first features of the world we label for children usually relate to properties of the physical world. Shapes, colors, numbers, animals, and different forms of transportation monopolize the toys and books designed for very young children.

Clearly, a child needs to be able to distinguish between red and yellow or a cow and a duck, and strong contrasts will always excite children's interest. However, it is telling that, in a society that struggles with the consequences of children's emotions, we often wait so long before we help children label their own feelings and those of others.

This may be because feelings seem a bit abstract and, therefore, potentially hard for a child to grasp. But, in fact, natural selection has already sensitized children to the emotional undercurrents of the world around them. However, to keep from being overwhelmed by the constant turmoil of feelings inside, children need to be able to organize and classify their emotional reactions. Giving them labels is an important start. Not only does the act of naming a feeling involve stepping back from it, thereby reducing its immediate intensity, but it leaves children in a position to start grouping and analyzing their emotional experiences. The human brain is remarkably good at searching for patterns. A reliable label will begin to clarify the circumstances under which the feeling in question occurs, ultimately helping your child decide which strategies are appropriate for dealing with it.

The A to Z of Emotions

In light of this, it is important to help children in their early years to become emotionally literate. You can do this in a number of ways. First, make an effort to attach appropriate verbal flags to your own feelings. When you are aware that your face and body are communicating an emotion, give it a name. Tell your child when you are feeling happy, sad, excited, confused, or playful.

For the reasons discussed previously, try not to expose your children to too much of your negative emotion. Having said that, because feelings such as fear, anger, and frustration need the most stringent management, being able to discern and identify such emotions is especially important. When you locate feelings of anger or distress using words, you demystify them and transform these states into mental objects that can be confronted and tackled. You are taking the first steps in helping your child tame the beast.

> Tell your child how *you* feel, to help him put a name to his emotions.
>
> # A B C

You can also help your child map out her emotional landscape by providing a commentary on the emotions that you observe your child experiencing. This needs to be done sensitively: If you misjudge a feeling state or are too quick to impose your own assumptions without reading your child's cues accurately, you may confuse matters. However, remarking that Toby "looks like a really happy and proud boy" when he approaches you beaming with his latest paint-splattered masterpiece is unlikely to be far off the mark. Similarly, commenting on Annie's "sad face" before offering comfort and a band-aid for her freshly grazed knee will begin to cement useful associations for her.

Although it's a good idea to avoid making dogmatic statements about what a child *is* feeling, it is perfectly legitimate to comment upon the emotional signals that your child is sending out. Making the observation that your son or daughter "seems angry" or "looks angry" instead of pronouncing that he or she *is* angry might seem like a subtle distinction. However, not only is the former more respectful (just note how irritating you find it the next time someone tells you what you're feeling), but the provisional nature of the observation also invites the child to check out whether what is happening inside matches the message being sent out. Ultimately, you want your child to be the foremost authority on the state of his own heart and mind. If you start taking that responsibility away from him at the outset of his life, you may be setting an unhelpful precedent.

> Don't tell a child how he is feeling, but do encourage him to tell you by making observations: "You look as if you are feeling angry."

Picture This

The level of difficulty even older children encounter in distinguishing among their emotions can be surprising. By the time we become adults, the distinctions seem self-evident, but this is not the case for a child whose mental experience is still largely unorganized. However, you can use the basic hard-wired connections between facial expressions and emotional states to help familiarize your child with different feelings.

You can help younger children with this task by using one of the commercially available sets of cards that depict a range of facial expressions. These present a variety of stylized emotions and can provide a useful aid for introducing your child to basic categories of feeling. Alternatively, you can simply cut out pictures from magazines. If you are feeling adventurous, you can use a digital camera to make your own customized "emotional mug shots" featuring family and friends and, of course, your child. The process of making these can be just as informative for children as the finished items, and the hapless, twisted faces of family members as they attempt various expressions usually makes this an entertaining project for all involved.

Use drawings or photos to discuss expressions and emotions.

Having a set of images available enables your child to move beyond the basic skill of identifying the different emotions. You can ask your child to pick out a card that represents the opposite of a target expression (happy as opposed to sad, calm as opposed to excited, and so on) or to begin grouping feelings that frequently occur together. The cards can also play a helpful role as an accompaniment to stories. You can ask your child to select expressions that correspond to the feelings a character might be experiencing in a particular situation: "How do you think Pooh felt when he got stuck in Rabbit's house? Let's pick out some cards that show us how he might feel...." This kind of tactic will not only develop a child's ability to empathize with the feelings of others, but it will also keep her more actively engaged.

Tell Me a Story

Whether or not you use expression cards as a prop, reading stories to your child is an important means of encouraging emotional literacy. The best-loved children's stories always take a character on some form of emotional journey, usually encouraging some level of identification from the listener. As with facial cues, good storytelling evokes the emotions it describes. Discussing with your children the motivations, experience, and reactions of major and minor characters is a painless and natural way to introduce them to a wide range of different emotional states. If the story is well written, the feelings depicted will relate to situations and events that your children can comprehend, making it possible for them to begin grasping the context of emotions and the circumstances likely to generate particular emotional reactions.

Read to your child and discuss how characters might be feeling. "Do you think he's feeling scared, angry, happy, or upset?"

Although you might think films and television programs offer similar opportunities, reading to your children has added value when it comes to promoting emotional literacy. There are a couple of reasons for this. When children are being read to, they need to do more of the mental work. They don't have the luxury of absorbing what they see in front of them. Instead, the words that they read (or are read to them) are a code that has to be actively unlocked by the child's imagination. Children must not only paint the picture in their mind's eye but they also must color it using their own feelings.

More importantly, the act of reading connects the thinking and feeling brain in a way that watching TV often does not. Written words stimulate multiple areas of the brain, producing an emotional response within the limbic system, but also activating networks of meaning in the cortex. The "cooling processes" that will ultimately enable children to soothe their own distress or calm their own anger rely on the part of the mind that deals in words. Stories that fuse feelings and meanings lay the foundation for personal control.

All Mixed Up

Me: So what are your feelings saying to you at the moment, Lisa?

[Lisa says nothing, but twists her hair between grubby fingers.]

Me: Okay, maybe that's too hard a question to answer right now.

[Lisa stares sullenly out of the window and says nothing.]

Me: Maybe we could talk a bit about your picture. This girl here in the beautiful green dress ... is she happy to be with her friends? I can't quite tell from the look on her face.

Lisa: I call her Spaghetti Girl. She's stupid.

Me: What an interesting name. Why is she called Spaghetti Girl?

Lisa: Because that's what she's like. Everything inside her is all squirmy and wormy and mixed up together.

Me: That sounds pretty messy—having everything jumbled up inside like that....

Lisa: *[conspiratorially]* Sometimes she wears a green dress. And sometimes she wears a red dress. And sometimes she wears a blue dress. And sometimes ... sometimes ... sometimes ...

Me: Yes?

Lisa: Sometimes that silly Spaghetti Girl wears all her dresses at once. And she gets *very* hot! *[giggles]*

This session with a six-year-old girl provided a telling insight into her emotional world. Lisa (not her real name) had plenty of reason to feel mixed up, like the girl in her picture. Her mother was struggling with a serious alcohol addiction and could switch very rapidly from being kind and caring at one moment, to becoming angry, aggressive, or withdrawn the next. Lisa never knew what she would find when she came home from school. She could end up baking by her mom's side or hiding behind a closed bedroom door while her mother ranted and raged in the hallway.

Lisa did what many children in such difficult circumstances do: She took her negative feelings about her unreliable caregiver and turned them in on herself to become the "stupid" Spaghetti Girl in her picture. However, although this exchange reflected a level of disturbance in Lisa's internal world, it also represented an important step forward. What Lisa was exploring is the notion that a person can feel more than one emotion at the same time.

The different-colored dresses worn by the unfortunate, mixed-up Spaghetti Girl stood both for the changeable nature of her mother and for the painful cocktail of conflicting feelings that Lisa held about her. She loved her mother but also feared her. She idolized her but secretly despised her behavior when she had been drinking. The fact that it was perfectly normal to hold such conflicting feelings about someone simultaneously was a revelation to Lisa. Like many children, she had initially assumed that feelings about things and people should be consistent and that she ought to feel one emotion at a time.

Lisa gradually realized that it is possible, and indeed perfectly normal, to experience a whole range of very different feelings about the same person. Even more importantly, she began to grasp that these contrasting feelings can coexist. Being able to separate and identify her different strands of feelings helped her impose some sort of order upon the noisy chaos of her internal world and feel less at the mercy of her emotions.

Although her case was extreme, some of Lisa's misconceptions about her feelings are common among children. As your child grows older, it is helpful to introduce the idea that it is possible to hold many feelings simultaneously and that our feelings are often jumbled up together, sometimes making it hard to know what is going on inside us.

Help your child to understand that you can be angry with somebody but still love them—it is possible to have more than one feeling at the same time.

An analogy helpful to some children is that identifying feelings is like learning to tune in to the different instruments in an orchestra. To demonstrate how this is done, you could listen with your child to the famous recording of Prokoviev's *Peter and the Wolf*, in which the narrator introduces each of the orchestra instruments individually, demonstrating how each instrument carries the signature theme of an animal in the story.

Beware of Buried Feelings

It is also worth explaining to school-age children that sometimes our feelings don't want to be put in the spotlight. Sigmund Freud's greatest insight was that it is our hidden feelings, the ones of which we are least aware, that can often have the most impact on our choices and behavior. In Freud's model of the human mind, many mental health problems result from the strain of stuffing painful or incongruent feelings below the level of consciousness. The enterprise of psychoanalysis aims to bring these submerged feelings into the light of day. By learning to acknowledge and tolerate the hidden fantasies and emotions that previously felt so alarming, Freud and his followers believed that they could release the damaging build-up of mental pressure. Freud viewed this process as fundamental to our emotional well-being.

It is certainly true that repressed feelings can cause difficulties for adults and children alike. Studies of particularly resilient children—those who deal well with life's setbacks—indicate that not only are they more able to articulate what they are feeling, but they also tend to be much more at ease with the full range of their emotions. They are able to acknowledge "difficult" feelings that other children find threatening.

For your child to feel confident about facing rather than evading his or her more disturbing emotions, it is necessary for you to give several clear messages.

First, you must let your child know that *no one is responsible for what they feel.* Our emotions are usually an automatic, gut response to a person or situation. Therefore, it makes no sense to blame someone for experiencing any kind of feeling, even a highly antisocial one. When your nine-year-old tells you he wants to rip the head off the little brother who has just tipped his football card collection on the floor there is no point reprimanding him or telling him he doesn't. Judging from the look in his eye, he really does. He is giving you (and himself) a very candid snapshot of what his emotions are telling him at that precise moment. Thankfully, those feelings can change.

Because we're not responsible for the feelings we experience, teach your children that they don't have to censor their emotions. In fact, we give emotions less power over us when we acknowledge them honestly. Denying feelings usually only makes them stronger. We may have to curb the way in which children *express* their feelings, especially if they start violating the boundaries of acceptable behavior (swearing at us or being deliberately offensive, for example). However, we must also give our children permission to hate, loathe, and despise us at times—however hard that can be for us, or however unjust it may feel.

For children to feel comfortable with not shutting off their feelings, the distinction must also be made—even to very young children—between *having* a feeling and *acting* on it. The message you need to broadcast repeatedly is that the urge to subject one's sibling to a slow and painful death is both natural and acceptable. Nevertheless, any action based on that desire is definitely not.

Tell your children that it's okay to feel whatever it is they feel...but it isn't always okay to act on that feeling.

This can be a surprisingly difficult distinction for even older children to grasp. Even into their early teens, children will plead the defense of provocation. When a child tells you, "She was annoying me, so I hit her," she might as well be telling you, "I released the ball, so it fell to the ground." In a child's mind, the emotional state induced (frustration) and the way it is expressed (violence) can become so closely identified that he loses any sense of ever having had a choice about his response. According to the magical thinking of children, feelings can actually make things happen. In your son's mind, his sister may as well have slapped herself after she started down the path of aggravation. The more children are able to register and identify feelings, building the detachment required to become their steward rather than their slave, the more choice they will have about how they respond to their emotions.

Shutting off problematic feelings appears to be second nature for young children, and they often need patient encouragement if they are to learn better ways of handling things and learn to tolerate feelings that make them feel uncomfortable or anxious.

Newton's third law of motion states that "for every action, there is an equal and opposite reaction." This is largely true of our feelings, which also tend to coexist in tension with their opposites. However, as the example of Spaghetti Girl Lisa reminds us, a child can find such contradictions especially hard to tolerate.

Children often respond by attempting to dispose of the feeling they don't want by repressing it. Child psychotherapist Melanie Klein argued that children learn to do this very early on to preserve an idealized mental model of the person who cares for them. This is because they can't afford to risk being dependent upon a mother or father who might let them down, even though sometimes this is unavoidable. Similar to Lisa, they try to bury the unwanted "bad" mother in their unconscious and hold on to the "good" one. Only in adolescence do most children feel robust enough to start dealing with their parents as real people, warts and all, whose imperfections no longer feel quite so dangerous. However, the free use of such primitive defenses does leave children particularly vulnerable to characteristic swings of feeling and attachment.

Getting the Feelings Out

Danny and Mike have been friends since playgroup. Most of the time they enjoy each other's company, but today there has been a serious falling-out. Mike returned home from school in tears, vehemently declaring that he *hates* Danny and *never* wants to see him again. In the post-mortem that follows, it becomes clear that Danny's transgression was pretty minor: He failed to bring in the action figure he had promised Mike could play with. But Mike will not be consoled. He is incandescent with fury.

A Russian Orthodox saying states, "The greatest virtues cast the longest shadows." Ironically, Mike and Danny's relationship has fallen prey to the very strategy that, until now, has ensured its success. Because Danny and Mike relied totally upon each other in the initially alien world of playgroup, they both worked hard to preserve an idealized vision of their friendship.

Danny unconsciously suppressed his irritation when Mike regularly invaded his personal space and got a bit physical when they were playing together. Mike chose to "ignore" how angry he felt every time Danny took his special toys off the shelf when he visited his house.

Although these two friends genuinely care for each other, under the surface unacknowledged resentments have been ticking away like a time bomb. Today the balance was accidentally tipped. Danny's moment of forgetfulness unwittingly unleashed years of buried resentment, which is why Mike now finds himself in the grip of such disproportionate fury.

Mike has fallen prey to what Freud called "the return of the repressed." If this occurs in the wrong way at the wrong time, the consequences can be devastating. Repressed material has a horrible habit of returning—often when we are stressed or least equipped to cope with it. Because children rely on basic emotional strategies such as denial and repression, they are particularly prone to triggering it. Although Mike and Danny's friendship will be saved and the fight will eventually be forgotten, it would have been better for both children if their latent irritation could have been identified and dealt with at the time. Unfortunately, neither child had developed the skills to do this.

When Mike's mother observed Mike tensing up each time Danny took his sacred toys down from the shelf, she told her son to "play nicely" and reminded him that it was part of being a good friend to share his toys. True enough, but it might have helped Mike if, after Danny had gone, his mother had observed, "It can feel quite hard when someone plays with your special things without asking." This would have allowed Mike to validate his feelings of resentment and prevented the toxic build-up of repressed emotion that nearly destroyed their friendship.

> If you notice your children being irritated, tense, or annoyed by the actions of somebody else (especially somebody they love), help them express those feelings instead of repressing them.
>
>

Heart to Heart: The Importance of Empathy

Mike and Danny's friendship was jeopardized by the accumulation of petty, unacknowledged resentments. However, the ultimate source of the problem was a repeated breach of empathy on both sides—Danny's indifference to Mike's feelings about his toys, and Mike's insensitivity to his guest's needs and desires.

Actress Meryl Streep, whose uncanny ability to inhabit the emotional lives of other people brought her Oscar-winning acclaim, once commented that the power of empathy is "the great gift of human beings." From a psychological perspective, she is completely right. Empathy is not just a moral virtue; it is also the most effective brake on children's bad behavior. Our ability to put ourselves in the shoes of others and attune ourselves sympathetically with their experience has been shown to help us clamp down on our more antisocial instincts.

Experimental findings offer increasing support for the view of the eighteenth-century German philosopher Arthur Schopenhauer, who concluded that "compassion is the basis of all morality." Ultimately, we want our children to behave because they appreciate the effects of their actions on other people. We don't want them not to bully, cheat, and steal because of the trouble they could get into, or even because subduing such urges wins them stickers, praise, or adulation. Deep down, we want children who avoid these things because they know they cause suffering to others.

Studies have actually demonstrated that fostering empathy skills is more likely to produce enduring pro-social behavior than punishments or bribes for good behavior. One researcher found that children rewarded for behaving well became so dependent on the rewards themselves that when the rewards were withdrawn, their behavior got worse. At the other end of the scale, criminals classified as sociopathic are among the most dangerous precisely because their lack of feeling for their fellow human beings makes them capable of almost anything. The message of the available research is this: If you want your children to be able to control their behavior, do all you can to help them become more empathetic.

> Encourage your child to be sensitive to the needs and feelings of others. "If you do this, how will he or she feel?"
>
>

Encouragingly, all the research evidence points to a strong link between children's capacity for empathy and their powers of self-control. Research has shown that children who score highly on impulse control measures are also more likely to demonstrate pro-social and empathetic behaviors.

Just because such a relationship exists between two factors does not, of course, mean that one has caused the other. Even if this were so, we have no way of knowing which is causing which. Maybe these children were more empathetic *because* they had better levels of self-control, rather than the other way around.

In fact, this might well be the case. Children who are better able to regulate their own emotional arousal may be better equipped to tune into others without becoming emotionally overwhelmed by their own responses. On the other hand, we know that children and young adults who are given empathy training do start behaving more considerately toward others— a result that suggests becoming more empathetic does enhance your powers of self-control in some situations.

The most likely explanation is that the two may be complementary—understanding that your actions might cause someone else pain gives you more motivation to hold back. And the ability to control your own emotions might put you in a better position to engage with other people's feelings.

You may also be interested to know that children who score high on empathy also tend to do better academically. As

Delores Gallo has noted, "It is not just moral reasoning, but reasoning generally which benefits from empathetic understanding." This might be because some of the skills related to empathy—including emotional regulation, perspective-taking, flexibility of thought, and capacity for reflection—also support learning ability. Whatever the connection, it gives all parents another good reason to nurture empathy.

The Expanding Heart

Some of the building blocks of empathy are laid at birth. We have already looked at the remarkable built-in ability of even very young infants to attune themselves to the emotions of those around them. You no doubt have encountered situations in which toddlers become infected with the feelings of their peers. When a young infant falls over and cries, you can bet that, before long, other toddlers around her will also be bawling. In fact, when one-year-olds were shown videotapes of crying children, most of them began showing signs of distress themselves—furrowing their brows, sticking out their lips, and sucking anxiously on their hands, their clothing, or a comforting toy. But is this really empathy in the true sense of the word? Instinctive mirroring might enable babies to replicate something of what others are feeling, but surely this is different from being able to appreciate the significance of those feelings for another person....

Around a child's first birthday, a significant change begins to take place. In a research project in which mothers were trained to spot and record empathetic responses from their children, by 13 to 15 months, more than half the children in the study showed signs of trying to hug or pat their mothers when they showed distress. By 20 months, their empathetic behaviors were becoming more sophisticated. The infants were bringing blankets, soft toys, and bandages to comfort their mothers, and even asking them if they were okay. By their second birthdays, they extended empathetic overtures to a wider circle, even including strangers.

Between two and three years of age, children become increasingly adept at spotting situations in which others are upset and offering support to them. We see them helping rebuild fallen towers, replacing broken crayons, and even spontaneously bringing bandages for bleeding fingers. Between the ages of six and eight, advances in children's cognitive abilities have put another vital piece in place. From this age, children are capable of proper perspective-taking—in other words, not only are they able to appreciate what someone else is feeling but also are better able to understand *why* they are feeling it. They have learned to see the situation through someone else's eyes.

Understanding just how early children are able to demonstrate empathy means that almost from birth, parents have a useful window of opportunity to nurture their child's empathy potential. As educationalist Charles Flatter reminds us, "Children come into the world predisposed to empathize with the feelings of other people but seem to lose the capacity if they are not encouraged to develop it." Unless we recognize how early children's capacity for empathy develops, we are unlikely to nurture it properly.

So what can parents do to support the growth of this most precious human talent? The growing body of research in this area has given us some clear pointers. As with all skills we want children to master, one of the keys is to demonstrate those skills ourselves so they can follow our lead. If our children have not felt understood, they will find it hard to extend understanding to others. For most children, their relationship with their parents gives them a template to imitate and reinforce the value of empathetic engagement.

> Show children how *you* are sensitive to the needs and feelings of others at every opportunity.

Strengthening the Bond Between You

The early months of a baby's life are often a master class in empathetic responsiveness. When you watch skillfully attuned mothers with their children, the interaction between them resembles a playful dance in which both parties seamlessly anticipate and respond to the actions of each other. The baby experimentally waves a toy in front of her own face, eyes widening in surprise; her mother responds by making an exaggerated expression of surprise of her own and simultaneously making soothing, cooing noises and maybe reaching out with a reassuring touch. The baby gurgles with pleasure and her mother responds by telling her in a lilting, sing-song voice that she is "such a clever girl." And on it goes.

Mothers who become adept at reading their baby's communications can tell what she needs and when—whether it be a feeding, a nap, or a diaper change—almost before the child consciously knows herself. But just as important, the baby learns to view the mother as someone who understands and anticipates her needs. This is her first experience of empathy, and it is a formative one.

One of the difficulties for mothers unfortunate enough to suffer from postpartum depression is that the relaxed rhythm of this formative dance between mother and child is disrupted. Various studies have shown that a sustained breach of empathy in the early months can have some consequences for a child's emotional, cognitive, and social development in the early years. However, it is reassuring that such differences tend to work themselves out as children mature if they have a supportive environment. The human brain is a remarkably plastic and adaptable organ, which means that we can keep on learning. When it comes to empathy training, it is rarely too late.

As your children grow older, their schooling in empathy depends increasingly on your ability to listen to them. It is very easy for parents to feel like air traffic controllers as they juggle the multiple demands of coordinating their children's school, social, and family commitments. Under such circumstances, many of us fall into a directive, businesslike, or even militaristic style of interacting with our kids—issuing our orders and demanding constant updates on whether they have remembered their gym bag, done their history project, or written that thank-you letter. Life can feel enormously busy, and under the weight of this pressure, "conversations" with our children can easily degenerate into a stream of commands and instructions. I know this only too well. Because you are so familiar with your children, it is easy to cut them off midflow or finish their thoughts and sentences for them. However, your child is unlikely to experience this as empathy—quite the opposite, in fact.

Make time to talk—and listen—every day.

However busy things get, be sure to still find time in your day to talk properly to your child and, more important, *listen* to what she has to say. Children who are able to share their problems with their parents and discuss their feelings become more empathetic toward others. But for this to happen, you have to create a climate in which this is encouraged:

■ Spend time together at a point in the day when both of you are likely to be relaxed. This might be just before bed or after a snack, depending on what fits best with your household routines.

■ Instead of formally sitting down with your child to "have a conversation," develop a routine activity or ritual (such as doing a crossword puzzle together with an older child) that provides a comfortable context in which such chats can take place. Boys, in particular, often prefer some notional joint task, to take the spotlight off their feelings.

■ During these times, learn to listen without interrupting or taking charge of the conversation. Always let your child finish what she has to say.

■ When your child is talking, pay attention. Look interested and be interested. Don't assume that you know what he is getting at. Show your child that you are actively listening by maintaining a good level of eye contact—usually about a third of the time as a rough guide—and using nonverbal signals such as nodding or dropping in the occasional "uh huh." These cues tell your child that you regard what he has to tell you as important and that you are doing your best to pay attention.

- When your child has finished telling you something, offer a brief paraphrase of what she has said. This will demonstrate that you have been listening and underline your desire to make sure you have properly understood your child's communication.

- Identify any implicit emotions in what your child is saying. "I imagine it must have really hurt your feelings when Justin said that to you...." Speculate rather than pronounce, but rest secure in the knowledge that when you get it right, you will be strengthening the empathetic bond between you.

By developing your own listening skills, not only will you help your child feel understood and improve your relationship, but you also will be modeling skills that your child will need to behave empathically toward others.

Getting the Balance Right

Some illuminating work has been done on the relationship between the development of empathy in the early years and the way in which parents express themselves. Several studies indicate that parents who demonstrate high levels of positive emotions through praise and enthusiasm are more likely to have children with high levels of empathy. Psychologists suggest that by helping children to experience and express emotion, these high levels of positive feeling help children become more at ease when it comes to experiencing other people's emotions.

The flip side of the coin is that if children are raised in a climate of intense negative emotion, they may become overaroused and experience real difficulties in learning about their own emotions, let alone those of others. Such children are unable to regulate their distressed feelings. They protect themselves by shutting off from others. Being met with threatening, rejecting, or inconsistent treatment by caregivers appears to have a similar effect.

> By displaying positive emotions, you are helping your child become more empathetic toward others.
>
>

On the other hand, it's not a good idea to wrap your infant in bubble wrap and protect him from anything negative. Allowing your child to witness some level of distress in others can actually help foster empathetic responses. The trick is not to expose your children to degrees of emotion (either negative or positive) that are too intense for them to handle. However, always try to ensure that the balance falls in favor of positive, upbeat, affirming emotions.

> Allow your child to see negative emotions, but in limited amounts. Don't let it become too intense—in either direction.
>
>

Fine-Tuning the Empathy Response

In addition to creating an empathetic environment at home, you can directly nurture your child's empathetic potential in other ways. The first is to notice and reinforce occasions when your child demonstrates empathy. When a child shows concern for someone else—your toddler attempts to console his howling playmate with an offer of a stuffed animal or your teenage daughter steps aside to let her friend have the last ticket to the concert—be on hand to affirm such behavior with your praise and respect.

When children do show empathy, and at those critical times when they don't, research indicates that it is a good idea to frame the incident in relation to their character rather than just their behavior. Emphasize that your child has done a kind thing because he has a kind nature—that's the sort of boy he is. Similarly, when he fails to show empathy appropriately, express your surprise as well as your disappointment because you know he's "not normally like that." Researchers have found that strengthening the notion that empathy is part of your child's natural character is likely to engender more empathetic conduct. The technical name for this process is "positive trait attribution," which is a fancy way of saying that the more strongly you define someone in a certain way, the more likely that person will be to act in line with the definition. However, make sure your attributions are realistic and credible.

> Tell your children they are kind and thoughtful, and always comment on behavior that supports this—or show surprise when it doesn't.
>
>

Discuss with your child how actions can influence feelings and prepare her for situations in which an empathetic response will be required. Explain that Grandma will be feeling tired and sore after her operation. Help your child think beforehand about what sort of behavior might be appropriate under such circumstances. Getting your child to role-play a situation from someone else's point of view has also proven to be a genuinely helpful method for helping children extend their empathetic understanding.

Studies with school-age children have shown that learning about examples of famously altruistic individuals—such as Mother Teresa, Albert Schweitzer, or Martin Luther King—can inspire them to cultivate their own powers of empathy. Also help your child become proficient at reading and interpreting nonverbal "body language." Let him know that an open palm facing upward is a sign of truth and honesty, that closed body language indicates that someone feels threatened, and that a head slightly tilted to one side signals attention but a head thrust forward is more likely to convey aggression. As your child matures, train him to spot the nonverbal leakage that can so easily provide clues to people's real feelings. There are many books that can help you both get started and find plenty of opportunity to practice honing your skills together.

Tell your child about people who are heroes for kind behavior and those famous for their exploits.

Finally, help your child avoid prejudice and the breakdown of empathy by emphasizing what your child shares in common with people who may appear very different. Projects that attempt to tackle racism in schools often begin by focusing on shared characteristics, traits, and goals before highlighting racial or cultural features that distinguish a particular group or nationality. The same strategy applies when your child encounters someone who is disabled or whose sexual orientation might be different from his own. Help your child realize that what he shares in common with other people far transcends anything that might set him apart.

> Make sure you highlight similarities between people before discussing the differences.
>
>

When we react with prejudice, empathy has already broken down. Prejudice always dehumanizes others, turning them into objects so that we stop seeing them as people similar to ourselves. If the human race was better at sustaining empathy, our children would be growing up in a more tolerant, less war-torn world. As with charity, empathy begins at home. The implications of raising empathetic kids are more wide-reaching than just ensuring a more peaceful life for us as parents.

One final caveat: Don't unwittingly perpetuate prejudice yourself by devoting more time to fostering empathy skills in your girls than in your boys. In Western culture, we tend to expect girls to be more empathetic than boys, and this can easily become a self-fulfilling prophecy. On almost every level, emotionally and cognitively, girls do usually mature earlier than boys who, on average—as far as I can gather—outstrip girls in tasks involving spatial navigation until their early teens. (Yes, it's true: Men are better at reading maps!) Boys are also more overtly aggressive than girls. For these reasons, it is even more important to hone their powers of empathy. In terms of these skills, boys are a vulnerable population—they really need your help.

Only Connect

If any further motivation were needed, perhaps we should conclude by focusing on one of the main findings from the Positive Psychology researchers. Human happiness depends in a large measure on our ability to form meaningful connections with others. This is a consistent finding in study after study. By employing the simple skills outlined in these pages, you will be able to increase your child's chances of enjoying a fulfilled, contented life. By helping your child understand the emotions of his own heart and training him to look into the hearts of those around him, you will be nurturing skills that will increase his chances of forming loving bonds that will sustain him throughout life. As the Dalai Lama put it, "If you want others to be happy, practice compassion. If you want to be happy, practice compassion." The emotional development of your children is a key to their future happiness as well as a cornerstone of well-regulated behavior.

Quick Summary Action Points

🌿 Make conscious efforts to help your child expand his emotional vocabulary:

→ Put clear, consistent labels on your own feelings.

→ Use real-life examples, pictures, and stories to identify and explain emotional reactions.

🌿 Help your child understand that it is possible to feel different and even contradictory feelings at the same time.

🌿 Teach your child to accept her feelings—even the less comfortable ones.

🌿 Be clear that no one is accountable for what they *feel*, only what they *do.*

🌿 Help your child not to bury feelings that can lead to problems later.

🌿 Encourage your child to become aware of the feelings and needs of others.

🌿 Work hard to show and encourage empathy, one of the cornerstones of self-control.

🌿 Give your child controlled exposure to positive and negative feelings, but keep the overall tone upbeat and affirming.

THREE

Mind Control for Beginners

Whether your child is two or a teenager, emotions running out of control can cause many headaches for parents—and it's not much fun for the child, either. Showing your children how to manage their thoughts, feelings, and actions puts them in control of a situation and gives them a real alternative to destructive behavior.

One useful set of techniques that can be used by grown-ups as well as children comes from Cognitive Behavioral Therapy (CBT). CBT has established a reputation as an effective form of "talking therapy" for a wide range of disorders from depression to anorexia. However, at its heart lies a cluster of principles and techniques that are relevant to all of us; you certainly don't need to have psychological problems to benefit from them. In essence, CBT is a way of putting the rational "cool" mind back in control when "hot" processing wreaks havoc with our lives. Therefore, it offers a very handy technology for dealing with destructive patterns of emotions and behavior.

The really good news is that the cognitive approach is child-friendly. The principles involved are simple enough for most school-age children to grasp, and its emphasis on practical, experimental learning fits well with the way most children operate. Unlike many therapies, CBT empowers people by equipping them with skills that they can apply in their lives. In fact, Martin Seligman, a professor at the University of Pennsylvania, has demonstrated that if you are schooled in the basics of CBT when you are young, these techniques can reduce your vulnerability to developing clinical depression.

Seligman is one of a number of influential psychologists trying to shift the discipline of psychology away from a focus on mental illness to consider instead the conditions that allow human beings to flourish and fulfill their potential. He views cognitive behavioral techniques not simply as a remedy for when things go wrong, but as an aspect of good mental hygiene that can protect people from getting sick in the first place.

This chapter focuses on how to encourage children to take greater responsibility for managing their emotions and how to give them simple techniques to do that. When children feel in control of their emotional life, chances are, their behavior will reflect this—and that means fewer headaches for both child and parent alike.

Attack of the Clowns: How We All See the World in Different Ways

Charlie, age four, and Tom, age six, are visiting the circus for the first time. Having cheered, gasped, and whooped its way through seven acts, the audience is now eagerly awaiting the arrival of Big Al and his sidekick, Little Mo. With a honk of a horn, an outlandish-looking car with wobbly wheels careers into the ring. Out of it burst the clowns. Big Al promptly trips over his giant shoes, sending Little Mo head over heels into a bucket of paste. Messy mayhem ensues.

Charlie finds this hysterical and almost falls off his seat with laughter. His older brother, Tom, is also hysterical, but, in his case, quite literally. The color has drained from his face and he is screaming uncontrollably. His parents can do nothing to console him and have to take him out of the performance. Tom goes on to develop a life-long phobia of clowns (*coulrophobia* is the official term) and has not been back to the circus since.

How do we begin to explain such completely different reaction to the same event? What ultimately determined the nature of each boy's response was not the event itself, but the very different ways in which it was perceived. Whereas Charlie embraced the whole sequence as a piece of entertaining, slapstick fun, for Tom, the performance tapped into something much more sinister. Each boy's emotional reaction was governed by what it meant to him.

What we feel is dictated not by what happens to us, but by the meanings we create around those events. No two people experience the world in exactly the same way, and your child may experience things differently than you. You can't tell children what to feel, but you can steer them toward interpretations of reality that are likely to promote their happiness.

> All children interpret events differently. You can't tell children what to feel, but you can help them find constructive ways to make sense of what happens to them.

I Think, I Feel, I Do

Our thoughts, feelings, and behavior are all connected and have a cumulative effect on each other. It stands to reason that if we change what we think about a situation, we might feel very differently about it too.

If I conclude that my friend deliberately ignored my wave as I passed by, I am likely to feel hurt and affronted. However, when I recall that the friend in question is short-sighted and wasn't wearing glasses at the time, this information puts a new spin on things.

The way we interpret an event determines not only our feelings, but also our subsequent behavior. A man lying in bed at night hears a noise downstairs. If he tells himself the noise was merely the cat going out of the cat flap, he is likely to roll over and go back to sleep. But if he assumes there is an intruder in the house, he might investigate further or call the police. Two different interpretations prompt two different behavioral responses.

Use daily events to show how there's usually more than one way of looking at things.

This can also work in the opposite direction. In some cases, simply changing behavior can also change the way people think and feel. For example, scientists have discovered that the mere act of deliberately putting on a smile actually improves people's subjective reports of happiness.

Shaping Your Child's Core Beliefs

When we find ourselves at the mercy of negative emotions, it's usually because we have managed to lose our sense of perspective—even if it doesn't feel like this at the time. Distressing feelings are usually primed by what psychologists refer to as "negative automatic thoughts." These are instinctive, irrational readings of situations that tap into our vulnerabilities. They often take the form of knee-jerk reactions and can be detected in those negative comments that pop into our heads at moments of distress: "She hates me," "I've messed it up again," "I'm making a fool of myself," and so on.

Although these self-critical thoughts usually relate to specific situations, they often reflect aspects of negative core beliefs. These are the more enduring, underlying convictions that sum up our feelings about ourselves and the world. The negative automatic thoughts cited previously might link into generic core beliefs such as "I'm unlovable," "Nothing I do is ever right," and "I'm worthless."

Once entrenched, core beliefs are difficult to shift and can exert a powerful influence on the way we live. As parents, therefore, it is particularly important that we do our best to ensure that our children construct healthy core beliefs about themselves.

We can do this partly through the explicit messages we give them. Every time we tell our children how much we love them, when we affirm our faith in them and demonstrate our pride in their accomplishments, we are helping program their core beliefs about themselves. Through our eyes, they learn to see themselves as people who are lovable and worthwhile. When we create opportunities for our sons and daughters to use their skills and talents, or support them in accomplishing their goals, we teach them that they are capable, effective individuals who can master life's challenges and are worthy of respect.

Make sure your children get plenty of positive feedback, and create opportunities for them to excel. This will help them construct healthy core beliefs.

Conversely, if we are constantly overly critical or reproving, we risk fortifying a child's secret fears: "Nothing I do is good enough," "I'm inferior," or even "I don't deserve to be loved." Children are especially receptive to information they get from the people they rely upon—and, unfortunately, we all have a natural tendency to pay more attention to bad news than good.

Just take a moment to think about the occasions when you're hardest on yourself. It's surprising how often at such times the inner voice of self-criticism or condemnation assumes the tones of an angry or disappointed parent. Even now, you may be able to recall particular parental statements or reactions that stung you badly and might even have shaped the way you see yourself.

Remember that the *repeated messages* you give your child will stay with them for life—make those things positive, not burdens your child has to carry.

Keep in mind that it is usually the overall tone and content of the messages we transmit to our children that mold their core beliefs. As in all relationships, we will say things to our children that we later regret. Rest assured, however, that no one-time statement will likely shape a child's view of himself. However, similar messages repeated day in day out will ultimately have an impact. Even things we don't necessarily mean can shape a child's self-image, so, when reprimanding your child, make every effort to label behavior as "bad" or "stupid" rather than your child. The power you have as a parent gives you a great opportunity to help children develop core beliefs that will pro-tect and fortify them throughout life. However, with that power comes the responsibility not to undermine their self-belief in moments of clumsiness, exhaustion, or irritability.

Seeing Only What Fits

Such is the power of our core beliefs that they act like a lens that filters our perception of reality. However reasonable we might think we are, unconsciously, we all have a tendency to remake the world in the image of our own convictions. We see what we are programmed to see. We might even act in ways that bring our experience into line with what we believe about ourselves, regardless of how helpful those beliefs may be for us.

We know, for example, that depressed people demonstrate certain thinking habits that will likely make them feel worse. For example, a depressed child will be highly selective about what she focuses on, usually attending only to facts that sup-port a negative view of herself and the world. She will stead-fastly ignore any information that does not fit in with those beliefs. She will be prone to "catastrophizing"—assuming that the worst possible outcome is the most likely in any situation, even if logic suggests that this is not the case. She will consistently blame herself for anything that goes wrong in her life, even events that are logically beyond her control. She will also make sweeping generalizations, asserting that any negative incident is "just typical" of the way she is.

And this isn't just about depressed children: All children have the ability to develop faulty thinking to reinforce what they believe about themselves. However careful you have been as a parent to instill positive core beliefs in your child, it's possible that they have formed some unhelpful ones of their own accord, or from things that friends or teachers have said. So if your child says things that seem odd to you, seems unhappy, or is losing control of herself, unhelpful core beliefs might be creeping in. Be alert and use the techniques described next to counteract them.

> Be alert to any signs that your child has negative beliefs about himself—in what he says or how he behaves.
>
>

Undoing Bad Thinking Habits

So how do you undo these sorts of bad mental habits and challenge the assumptions that underlie them? The main solution is through careful and deliberate examination of the evidence supporting the negative assumption. As in a courtroom, your child needs to learn how to present the case for and against his thoughts and evaluate them in light of the factual evidence. Even relatively young children can successfully learn to evaluate their destructive assumptions in this way.

When a child loses control of her behavior, you can bet that powerful feelings are working in conjunction with a cascade of negative assumptions that compound until the point of meltdown. Children often overreact because they give in to catastrophic interpretations of what is happening to them. They often lose sight of the bigger picture, get swallowed up in the intensity of their own distress, and disconnect their immediate experience from wider webs of meaning that otherwise would provide an emotional safety net. Furthermore, children often see their own destabilized emotions as further evidence of the truth of their upsetting thoughts.

Picture a nervous toddler who has wandered off in a department store and lost sight of his mother. Although he probably can't articulate his thoughts explicitly, the mental process he experiences would probably look something like the following:

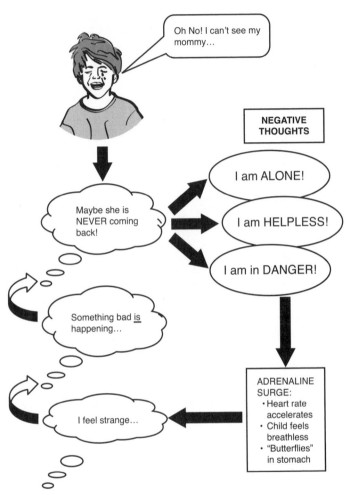

You can easily see how this catastrophic cycle of thought and feeling can escalate. Before long, this child will be reduced to a state of extreme distress. Of course, when his mother does find him again, he will have a new experience that hopefully will weaken the assumption that briefly losing contact with his parent means he has been abandoned.

Teaching your child to challenge negative thinking and keep a cool head isn't something you can achieve overnight. However, the ability to neutralize upsetting thoughts is very useful for a child and can become the foundation of a robust self-image. This will also help put your child back in the driver's seat of his emotions—at least, in theory. In the next few sections, we explore how you can apply the cognitive approach in practice and, more important, teach your child to do the same.

Connecting the Dots

To children, the fact that their thoughts affect their feelings and vice versa is not necessarily obvious. Yet this is a connection that children need to be introduced to as early as possible, to limit the impact of negative thinking.

> Take every opportunity to show your child how changing the way you think can change the way you feel.
>
>

You can introduce this concept to a school-age child in a number of low-key ways. Making explicit connections between what people think and what they feel is something you can do in a number of everyday situations. This mainly involves picking up on opportunities in everyday conversation with your child. Say, for example, that your son reports seeing another child crying on the playground during recess. Typically, these kinds of conversations go as follows:

Child:	I saw Matthew crying on the playground at recess today.
Mother:	Did you, darling? What made him upset?
Child:	I don't know. I think it was because Gary and Roger didn't play football with him like they normally do.
Mother:	That's a shame. Maybe you could ask him to play with you?

Although the mother helpfully offers a solution, demonstrating some basic problem-solving skills, she misses the opportunity to challenge her son's assumption that events—rather than their interpretation—produce emotions. The same conversation could have been handled as follows:

Child:	Matthew was crying on the playground at recess today.
Mother:	Was he, darling? Why *do you think* he was so unhappy?
Child:	I dunno. Probably because Gary and Roger didn't play football with him like they normally do.
Mother:	Oh dear! *So what did Matthew think of that*?
Child:	Well, probably that they didn't like him anymore.
Mother:	Hmm, well if that's what *he was thinking,* I can see why he might have felt sad. But aren't the three of them friends? Was there some other reason why they didn't play with him today?
Child:	Maybe because he was late out after class and they thought he was swapping football cards with Mike like he did yesterday.
Mother:	Did anyone point that out to him? How do you think Matthew would have felt *if he had realized* that was the reason?

Child: I guess he probably wouldn't have been so upset. What's for lunch?

Prompting children to make connections between what other people think and feel in everyday situations lays a valuable foundation for handling their own difficult feelings.

Gently challenge your child's assumptions about other people's feelings. "Why do you think he felt that?" "Could there have been another reason he was sad?"

Using TV and Books

Stories that involve elements of disguise or deception are particularly handy for making this association. They underline discrepancies between what a "misled" character believes and the reality of the situation.

In the children's cartoon *Scooby-Doo*, a team of not-so-fearless detectives are regularly called upon to investigate sightings of a ghost or monster. The format of each episode dictates that the appearance of said ghost provokes much histrionic behavior—especially from the hapless Shaggy and Scooby, who spend much of the episode racing down corridors with the "ghost" in hot pursuit. At the denouement of each episode, the supernatural fiend is unveiled, usually turning out to be Mrs. Delaney, the vengeful aunt, or Hector, the embittered gardener. The cast breathes a collective sigh of relief and the credits roll.

As usual, their unfounded fear was based upon a misperception. This is a point that can be made to even young children:

"What did Shaggy feel when he *thought* it was a ghost?" "What did he feel when he *realized* it was just a man with a sheet on his head?" Simple questions like these introduce children to the notion that what people feel and do is strongly influenced by what they believe.

Using Drawings

You can also introduce the relationship between thoughts and feelings using drawings of stick figures with blank faces and thought bubbles. Give your child a scenario and ask her to come up with a corresponding thought. Then invite her to draw the expression that goes with what the figure is thinking. For example, Joanna, the stick figure in the picture, might have just been told she is going to the zoo that afternoon. Most children will put a positive cognition in the thought bubble: "I am a lucky girl," "The trip will be fun," "Today is a happy day," etc. When asked how that thought makes Joanna feel, they will obligingly draw a smile on her face.

The next stage is to demonstrate what happens to Joanna's feelings when events take a turn for the worse. Perhaps when they arrive, the zoo is closed, or while walking around she drops her ice cream. The process is repeated, usually eliciting a negative thought ("Everything's spoiled") and a sad face. At each stage, the adult makes the link between what Joanna is thinking and the emotions she is experiencing.

The final phase is to present the child with another stick figure on which the adult draws a neutral or more cheerful expression. The child is asked, "Can you think of *anything* that we can put in this thought bubble that might make Joanna's face change from *this* [indicates "sad" Joanna] to *this* [pointing to image of a more cheerful/neutral Joanna]?"

With a little encouragement, most children will volunteer a more upbeat thought involving a shift in perspective or even a solution to the problem. Examples might include "We can always come back tomorrow when the zoo is open" or "My daddy will buy me another ice cream, so it doesn't matter." The quality of the content is not that important. What is vital is that the child begins to understand that what goes on in her head directly influences what she feels.

When using this technique at home, you have the advantage of being able to use an example directly from your child's own experience, maybe at the very time this is most relevant. Using drawings makes it a relaxed and familiar way of raising the subject.

> Use stick figures and thought bubbles to show the connection between thoughts and feelings, and how thinking something positive can make you feel happier.
>
>

Trapping Negative Thoughts

Spotting our habitual negative thoughts can prove tricky for adults and children alike, but this is an essential skill to master. Many of these thoughts have been so well-rehearsed in our heads that we are barely conscious of them as thoughts at all. As with the wallpaper that we no longer notice when we enter a room, our negative thoughts can assume a taken-for-granted quality that can render them all but invisible. They also flit through consciousness so quickly that it can be hard to isolate them.

In the case of children, cognitive immaturity means that their subjective readings of reality can all too easily take on the status of undisputed fact: "No one likes me ... that's just the way it is." Seeing himself in this way, Alec screens out the time Richard and Mike invited him to join them on the trip to the movies. Carrying this belief with him, when Alec does find himself in social situations, he doesn't think he's welcome. He expects rejection and copes either by holding back or by alienating other children before they can reject him. Thinking and behaving in this way make it harder for Alec to make friends and see himself in a different light. The problem is now perpetuating itself.

A child in Alec's situation needs support to understand and break the cycle in which he has become trapped, and some of the techniques we will look at will hopefully show how that can best be achieved. However, Alec also needs to be encouraged to shift the focus away from himself. Learning to show an interest in other people and appreciate what he has to offer in social situations will equip Alec to collect fresh evidence that he can then use to challenge his negative assumptions about himself. Chapter 6, "People Powers: Cultivating Social Confidence," offers some more tips about how to handle relationships with other children.

Know Your Enemy

To help younger children identify negative thoughts, it can be useful to give their source a concrete, visual representation. In Western culture, we are all familiar with the image of the devil and the angel at our shoulder, each trying to grab our attention. Your child needs to know that we all have a "saboteur," or part of ourselves that is hell-bent on making our lives miserable. This invisible enemy is the source of negativity, pessimism, destructive criticism, and all those thoughts that make it hard for us to feel very good about ourselves.

I often ask children age five and older to invent a character who will give their saboteur some sort of tangible form. Younger children struggle with abstract concepts but most will happily engage with the task of drawing a picture or making a model of their saboteur.

You can introduce the idea as follows:

> "Most of us have a voice in our head that can say really mean things to us and make us feel sad and worried. Can you give me an example of some of the sorts of things that voice might say to you? [Prompt with your own example if the child is finding it hard.] I want you to imagine the sort of person or creature who might be saying those types of things to you. Let's pretend that this voice in your head also has a body. What sort of creature or thing do you think it might be? It's your creature, so you can make it anything you want...."

Some children create monsters or witches; others come up with thunderclouds or animals. By all means, respond to the emotional qualities of what your child depicts ("Gosh, those claws look sharp!"; "The fact you can't see her face makes her look quite spooky...."), but be careful not to impose your own assumptions or start adding your own ideas. Instead, follow your curiosity and use open questions to encourage your child to flesh out his creation. Younger children will need these questions to be quite concrete:

➤ Where does he/she/it live?

➤ What sort of things does your monster like doing?

➤ How do its weapons work?

83

It goes without saying that you'll need to modify this approach for older children, although the concept of a personal saboteur is still one that many teenagers (and adults, for that matter) find appealing. For teenagers and older children who might find this all a bit babyish, you can draw useful analogies with computers. For example, you can compare negative automatic thoughts to computer viruses that are capable of corrupting system software and causing malfunctions.

When a child is struggling with negative thoughts, get her to draw or model the "baddie," the character who whispers the negative things to her. Then show her how to defeat the baddie by choosing to ignore its tactics.

Although most people experience negative thoughts in the form of subliminal "voices" in their heads, some individuals also experience these thoughts in a more visual form, perhaps picturing themselves failing or seeing their worst-case scenario playing out in their mind's eye.

When your child has established what form his saboteur will take, the next step is to give it a name. After that, you need to think with your child about its armor and the tactics that it uses to make her feel bad. The easiest way to do this is to think about the kind of things the saboteur typically says when it wants to make your child feel sad, worthless, or anxious. What your child comes up with in response to this can often provide you with important insights into the nature of your child's fears. The Ugly Monster might tell John that he is a "pathetic weakling," or the Dinosaur of Doom might growl at Jenny, "No one will ever want to be your friend."

When you have collected an adequate sample of critical self-statements, you can examine them together and see whether you can discover any clues about the way the saboteur operates. With a little luck, you will be able to establish several important principles: What the saboteur tells you is almost always a distortion of the truth. Your saboteur is a liar. And it doesn't play fair. However, you also need to let your child know that she is powerful enough to defeat it.

At this stage, the important thing is that your child is learning to articulate and group together self-statements that share a common quality. By learning to recognize the distinctive "voice" of their personal saboteur, children can start to differentiate between thoughts that are helpful and those that are less so. A category of "bad" thoughts is created that your child knows must be approached with caution.

As your child learns to equate negative thoughts with the activity of the saboteur, she is already beginning to bracket such thoughts and no longer accept them at face value. She is learning to identify self-defeating tendencies in herself and familiarize herself with the ways they undermine her self-esteem.

Personifying your child's negativity in this way gives you both an accessible, common language to talk about fears and destructive thought patterns. Being able to think with your child about where a specific thought comes from ("Is Terrorix trying to slip in another thought bomb to make you feel bad, honey?") is a helpful way of getting a child into the right mindset. Framed in this way, your child will also readily understand why the enemy's schemes must be met with active resistance.

The Monster Disposal Squad

A further advantage for children who are too young to challenge the saboteur's statements using an analytical or rational strategy is that, by giving their negativity a tangible form,
they can use simple visualization techniques to help counter its
effects. A boy whose saboteur took the form of a fire-breathing
dragon imagined himself with a magic suit of armor that
reflected the blast back toward its source whenever it tried to
make him feel afraid. A six-year-old girl I knew equipped herself with a large vacuum cleaner to suck up her "angry blue
cloud." Shrinking the saboteur down until it can be popped in a
matchbox is popular, and children often invent imaginative
(and often quite violent) technologies to silence the voice of
their inner critic.

Although this isn't the same as being able to unpick negative
thoughts in the way they can when they get older, being able to
picture themselves taking charge of the situation gives many
children a sense of control over thoughts and feelings that
would otherwise overpower them.

What's the Damage?

Once a negative thought has successfully been identified, the
next stage is to look at its emotional impact. If you've used the
techniques in Chapter 2 to sensitize your child to different feelings, detecting and labeling the resulting emotions shouldn't
be too difficult. However, when you're attempting to apply cognitive strategies to manage feelings, it is also very helpful to

try and rate their intensity. This provides a good test of any antidote thoughts your child generates later. Does the antidote thought effectively reduce the force of the original emotions? Unless you've rated this, you'll have a hard time telling.

To show how this works, consider the example of Tabitha, who is nine years old. It is dinnertime, and, uncharacteristically, Tabitha has been in a foul mood since she returned home from school. She has been tormenting her little sister mercilessly and fighting with her brother over who gets to control what they watch on TV. Her mother doesn't know what has gotten into her and is swiftly approaching the limits of her patience.

However, instead of shouting at her, she takes Tabitha aside, gives her some frank feedback about her behavior, and asks whether she can think of any reason why she's finding it so hard to behave herself. Tabitha reminds her mother that tomorrow is the day of her Grade Three piano exam. Although she has been working conscientiously toward this for months, it seems that Tabitha is suffering from a last-minute crisis of confidence.

Ask a badly behaved child to think of any reason he's finding it hard to behave like normal today. If the answer turns out to be a worry, explore the negative thoughts behind it.

Working together, Tabitha and her mother brainstorm several negative thoughts that might be fueling Tabitha's anxiety and bad behavior:

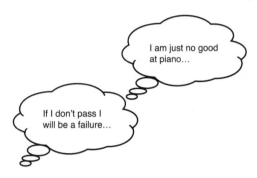

Out of these three, the last thought appears to be the most relevant because it is producing the strongest emotional reaction. This is Tabitha's "hot thought," and her rating of the emotions it generates in her is shown here:

Hot Thought	Emotion	Rating
"If I don't pass I will be a failure."	Afraid	4 / 10
	Miserable	7 / 10
	Helpless	8 / 10
	Angry	5 / 10

The process of gauging the strength of the feelings is an important stage in engaging the more objective "cooling" centers of the brain. Emotions are being experienced, but also considered and quantified. Younger children will obviously require a simplified scale (a little/quite a bit/a lot) and teenagers can usually handle percentages. However, the principle is the same.

Teach your child to rate the intensity of his feelings: "If 1 is not angry at all and 10 is the angriest you can imagine, how angry are you?"

Looking at the breakdown of Tabitha's feelings, it becomes easier to understand why she had been throwing her weight around with her siblings. Asserting her dominance was one way of compensating for her underlying feelings of vulnerability.

Sometimes your child might not be aware of the buried hot thought that is driving his emotions, or the negative thoughts identified may feel a bit tenuous. You can use the "downward arrow" technique to bring your child closer to the thought that is really driving his anxiety. This simply involves probing each thought or aspect of the situation and exploring their implications using simple questions:

➤ What would be the worst thing about that?

➤ What does that mean for you if that is true?

➤ Why would that be so terrible?

Repeat this process with each answer, to peel back the layers and get closer to the core anxiety. In the following example, Harry's negative automatic thoughts are in bold type:

Harry:	I don't want to go to school today.
Parent:	Why is that? What's so bad about today?
Harry:	We've got that geography test.
Parent:	Why is that such bad news?
Harry:	Well, **I'm bound to screw up again**.
Parent:	And if you do? What will happen?
Harry:	Umm ... well, **everyone will laugh at me**.
Parent:	Okay. That doesn't sound great, but what would be the hardest part of that for you if it did happen?
Harry:	It means **I'm dumb**.

Parent:	Well, I certainly don't agree with you on that one— but let's pretend it's true for a moment: Why does being smart matter so much?
Harry:	Well, who wants to be friends with an idiot? [**If I am stupid, no one will like me.**]
Parent:	But do you feel that no one likes you at school?
Harry:	Sometimes.
Parent:	What would that mean about you if it was true?
Harry:	Maybe that **I'm just no good**.

You can see how using the downward arrow technique made it possible to get closer to the real hot thought that was making Harry reluctant to go to school. The anxieties about his academic performance were a bit of a red herring. Harry's underlying problem was his perception that he was unpopular and his distorted belief that people with few friends must, by definition, have something wrong with them.

Weighing the Evidence

The next stage is to help your child evaluate the truth status of the negative thought. As in a court of law, you do this by carefully weighing the evidence that supports the negative thought against other information that might discredit it. Explain to your child how the legal system works, and tell her that she will need to play the role of both prosecution and defense attorney to establish whether a "thought crime" is being committed.

First, invite your child to think about the various factors that make the negative belief seem true. Has she had similar experiences that reinforce that belief? Are the factors emotional, or are there any logical or common-sense grounds to support it? At this stage, resist the temptation to start analyzing whatever your child says. Let the reasons all come out. It's important to have a genuinely open mind: If there are grounds to take the belief seriously, these need to be given due weight. This approach works only if you're both honest. Try and brainstorm as comprehensive a list as possible.

Having gathered the evidence in support of the belief, your child needs to draw up a second column. This time she is cast into the role of prosecutor. This second list should include anything that contradicts or challenges the authority of the negative belief. Are there any rational grounds on which to object to the belief? Has your child had *any* experiences that appear to contradict it? If so, it cannot be completely true. Are there reasons to suggest that the belief is too extreme or represents a biased view of reality? It will be very helpful if your child has become familiar with the common thinking errors in the box below. Our negative beliefs often reflect these kinds of distortions, and familiarity with them naturally makes them much easier to spot.

Work with your child to find examples or evidence that *supports* the negative belief—and then ask her to think of evidence or examples that suggest it's *not* true.

If your child is finding it hard to pick apart the negative thought, a useful strategy can be to ask him to think about what a friend might say about the belief or whether the belief would be endorsed by someone (real or fictional) your child admires: "Do you think that Uncle Dave would see it that way, Luke? What would *he* have to say about it?"

Some Common Thinking Traps to Watch Out For

➤ **Catastrophizing**—Assuming the worst and seeing the consequences as more terrible than they need to be. ("I've made a complete fool of myself. I won't *ever* be able to show my face in there again.")

➤ **Mind-reading**—Ascribing motives, intentions, and judgments to other people without any real evidence. ("They're bound to all hate me now." "He obviously tripped me on purpose.")

➤ **Overgeneralizing**—Making sweeping statements and assumptions on the basis of a single incident. ("I've missed the bus. Why does everything *always* go wrong for me?")

➤ **Selective perception**—Looking at only the facts that support your prejudiced view. ("He wasn't smiling, so I've obviously upset him.")

➤ **Using emotive language**—Putting things in exaggerated or graphic terms that make them seem worse than they are. ("I'm such an *idiot.* No wonder people *can't stand* me.")

➤ **Setting unrealistic expectations**—Making distorted assumptions about what should happen in a situation, often leading the person to take excessive responsibility or set unrealistic standards of behavior for themselves or others. ("I *should* have seen it coming." "He *ought* to have done much better than that." "I *must not* fail again.")

➤ **Personalizing**—Taking things personally, even when events are just the result of chance or bad luck. ("And now my dog needs an operation. Someone up there has really got it in for me.")

> ➤ **Thinking in black and white**—Seeing things in polarized "all or nothing" terms. ("If they don't agree with me, they must be my enemy." "If I don't come in first, I'll be a failure.")

In her capacity as prosecutor, your child is also entitled to cross-examine the defense witnesses. This means that she needs to look carefully at the statements in the first column and see whether she can spot any flaws in the argument and inconsistencies or logical weaknesses. These are added to the case against the negative thought. In Tabitha's example, her final list of evidence "for" and "against" looked like this:

Belief in the dock: "If I don't pass, I will be a failure."

Evidence For (Things Telling Me My Belief Is True)	Evidence Against (Things Telling Me My Belief Is Untrue)
My strong gut feeling that my belief is true.	My feelings cannot always be trusted. (Remember how I had a crush on Robin Wainwright in second grade!)
Ellie Jones is really successful and has passed her eighth-grade violin class already.	Even successful people make mistakes and get things wrong sometimes.
Mrs. Roddick says that anyone can do *anything* if they try hard enough. I have tried really hard, so if I still fail, that must mean I'm not as good as most people.	Making mistakes is part of learning something. All success involves some failure along the way. Mrs. Roddick was just trying to make us all believe in ourselves.
I certainly felt like a failure last time when I messed up my bicycling proficiency and nearly everyone else in the class did really well.	But even though I didn't do that well compared with the others, I still passed. In fact, two other people didn't do as well as I did—I think Sue actually failed the test.
I knew I was going to do badly in the race on sports day, and that turned out just how I thought it would.	Even if I fail my third-grade test tomorrow, it won't be the end of the world. My family will still love me, and I'll still have my friends and lots of things I'm good at and enjoy. Perhaps I need a different definition of success?

Evidence For (Things Telling Me My Belief Is True)	Evidence Against (Things Telling Me My Belief Is Untrue)
Lots of people are better than me at piano.	It's crazy to see myself as a "success" or a "failure" based on just this one thing.
Everyone will be really disappointed in me if I do fail.	I can only do my best. If I need to, I can always take it again. I will probably be the most disappointed, and I don't need to make myself responsible for other people's feelings. Anyway, the people I love have never minded that much when I have messed up in the past.
Granddad always says you are either a winner or a loser in life. Winners don't mess things up.	I have practiced hard and my music teacher says I'm ready. It's probably only my fear telling me I won't pass. Chances are, I will. In the worst-case scenario, I can take it again.

Any Other Offers?

Having reviewed all the evidence for and against, your child needs to see whether he can come up an alternative thought that more accurately reflects the newly perceived truth of the situation. This needs to be a *realistic* thought based on working through all the various arguments. Simply replacing the negative belief with idealized, wishful thinking won't have any impact on your child's emotions. It has to ring true.

The more adaptive thought may be taken straight from one or more of the elements in that second column, or it might simply be a modification of the original thought that acknowledges some elements of "second column" thinking. Some of the reasons given in the second column may be much more pertinent than others.

Tabitha's eventual antidote thought was as follows:

> Failing one exam will *not* make me a failure as a person, however badly I want to pass. None of the most important things in my life will change if I do fail. I don't have to be perfect at everything to be a good person.

At the end of this process, Tabitha rated her new belief as having a strength of 8 out of 10. She then tested the effectiveness of this new thought by rerating her original feelings as honestly as possible.

Emotion	New Rating
Afraid	2 / 10
Miserable	1 / 10
Helpless	2 / 10
Angry	2 / 10

Review all the points for and against the belief being true and see if together you can find a new belief—one based on the evidence. This is the antidote thought.

Troubleshooting

For Tabitha, her new antidote thought produced a marked reduction in the strength of her unpleasant feelings. However, if you find that your child's emotion ratings aren't shifting significantly, check out the following:

➤ Did you identify the relevant hot thought(s) in the first place?

➤ Has your child really grappled with the evidence for and against—or is he giving himself (or you) pat answers based on what he ought to think or what you want to hear?

➤ Are more powerful underlying beliefs or core assumptions fueling the problem that need to be addressed directly?

➤ Does the new alternative thought reflect the truth of the situation rather than a sanitized version of it?

Over to You

Although the principles of the cognitive approach are quite straightforward, consistently applying the techniques to real-life situations predictably proves more challenging for some children. The cognitive behavioral approach is more than a rag bag of techniques: It's also a mental discipline. Establishing it as a consistent part of your child's orientation to life requires coaching and support.

To begin with, the whole processes of identifying and appraising automatic thoughts can seem a rather long-winded business. However, please don't be tempted to skip stages—you'll weaken the usefulness of the technique if you approach it in a haphazard manner. As with many other skills that are painful to acquire in their early stages, these strategies will come to feel much more natural and spontaneous in time. Eventually, your child will be able to perform these stages in her head.

When a child sees a professional for therapy, the time available is usually quite limited. Within the scope of just a few weeks, the child must be introduced to the cognitive behavioral model, taught the necessary techniques, and given tasks and home-work relevant to the target problem.

As a parent, however, you are in an enviable position. You not only have time on your side, but you also have a privileged insight into the struggles your child faces on a daily basis. You have countless opportunities to help your child make sense of these situations and reactions to them. You can be there "in the field" to gently prompt and remind, to reinforce your child's efforts and gently pick her up when she's struggling to apply the techniques. All of this is hard work. But if you stick with it, you will see results.

> Take every opportunity to identify and examine negative thoughts. In time, you'll be able to do so more quickly and eas-ily, and eventually your child will do it automatically without your prompting.
>
>

When your child gets good at this process, you will see the ben-efits start to manifest in your child's behavior. Most children who learn these techniques become less prone to panic in the face of distressing feelings and less inclined to "act out" as a way of coping with them. They stop taking their fears at face value because they have a reliable strategy for dealing with their emotions. Being less at the mercy of their feelings gives young people more choice about how they will respond to them. And that's important.

Quick Summary
Action Points

～ What we feel about any event, and how we react to it, depends on our interpretation. Don't assume that your child sees things as you do— or as his siblings do.

～ Use everyday situations to teach your child the connections between thoughts, feelings, and behavior. Ask questions such as "Why do you think?" and "How did that make you/him feel?."

～ Watch out for negative and biased thinking in your child's way of looking at herself and the world.

～ Help your child recognize that upsetting thoughts usually involve a distortion of reality.

～ Encourage your child to give a concrete form to his inner saboteur. Personifying the source of your child's negative thoughts can make the task of doing battle with it less daunting.

～ Practice cognitive strategies with your child to analyze and manage distressing feelings:

  ↪ Teach her how to identify destructive hot thoughts.

  ↪ Show him how to review the evidence both for and against.

  ↪ Enable your child to become skilled at generating more balanced alternative thoughts.

FOUR

Becoming Indestructible:
Nurturing Resilience in Young People

For most parents, the idea of a child being depressed or anxious is hard to imagine. We either think it won't happen to our children or we dismiss the idea that such well-cared-for children could become depressed. What we can't ignore is that numerous painstaking studies have clearly shown that depression not only is endemic, but also is striking earlier and earlier.

Good parenting means being aware that depression happens, being ready to deal with it if it does, and, most of all, actively putting in place strategies to prevent it. After all, if you have it in your power to give your child the best possible chance of a healthy mind as well as a healthy body, why wouldn't you?

We all need to pay attention to the childhood depression figures because depressed and anxious states of mind can often be the root cause of "bad behavior." Parents need to be mindful of this possibility both when confronting such behavior and when putting in place strategies to deal with it.

Fortunately, we can do much to instill mental habits that can protect children against developing conditions such as depression and anxiety. In this chapter, we look at some of the key principles behind these good habits and show how you can encourage your child to cultivate them.

Spotting the Problem

General practitioners sometimes refer to depression as the common cold of psychiatry, but this analogy hardly does justice to the incapacitating impact that clinical depression and anxiety can have on people's lives. People who suffer from depression don't merely feel "down" and find it hard to motivate themselves. The condition can also affect concentration, memory, and sleeping and eating patterns. Depressed people can become withdrawn and irritable, and feel hopeless or full of self-loathing.

In children, depression is often missed because it doesn't always resemble its adult counterpart. Because of the way children handle emotional turbulence, instead of becoming classically flat and withdrawn, a depressed child might become more aggressive, rude, or generally difficult to manage. The first signs of depression might be reports of misbehavior or poor performance at school.

Alternatively, depressed children may respond by regressing or translate their emotional distress into physical symptoms—stomach complaints, headaches, and other aches and pains. Disturbed nights or recurrent nightmares could be another warning sign that's something is awry. As a parent, it is worth familiarizing yourself with the symptoms in the following box.

Depression Checklist

☐ Exhibits a lasting low, sad mood that doesn't shift

☐ Seems unusually touchy, irritable, or angry

☐ Complains of feeling worthless: "I am bad." "I am stupid." "No one likes me."

☐ Seems flat: loses interest in preferred activities

☐ Starts sleeping more or has disturbed nights

☐ Puts on or loses weight

☐ Finds it hard to concentrate and remember things

☐ Becomes either sluggish or constantly "on the go"

☐ Reports thoughts or dreams of dying or suicide

Of course, just because your child is behaving badly doesn't necessarily mean that he is depressed or stressed. However, if such behavior is unusual, it's always worth considering whether this might be the case.

Where Do We Draw the Line?

Even if it were possible to guarantee that your child would never suffer from a diagnosable depression or anxiety disorder, the information in this chapter is still relevant to you. In the West, our disease approach to mental health encourages us to bracket off such states as identifiable illnesses. We have a whole system of diagnostic criteria to draw a clear line in the sand between "normal" experience and an official mental illness. For example, to qualify for a formal diagnosis of clinical depression, you have to feel down most of the day or stop enjoying things consistently for at least a two-week period, as well as present a selection of other symptoms.

However, although they serve a purpose, these diagnostic cut-offs also disguise the fact that conditions such as depression and anxiety are also spectrum disorders. We all feel down at times. Sometimes we find ourselves in a blue funk that may even last for days. We all get anxious and jittery or have periods during which we know we're approaching the end of our rope and even notice ourselves worrying obsessively about certain things.

Normally, these episodes pass. We bounce back, and our symptoms have been neither severe nor sufficiently enduring to earn a formal diagnosis. However, although our experiences during those times may be less intense and extreme than that of a card-carrying depressive, there's probably more overlap than we'd like to believe. Most of us are quite good at deleting the bad times, especially if our reactions during them feel uncharacteristic, but even the least depressed and anxious of us have periods when we feel like depressed or anxious people—and, more important, start thinking like them.

All children can have times of feeling depressed or anxious, even if that isn't a permanent state.

Children, in particular, are capable of shifting into different moods and states of mind very rapidly. As we all do, they can inhabit depressed or anxious states without ever reaching the threshold for diagnosis. While they occur, these "micro episodes" can still have an effect upon your child's behavior. Unless your child learns to tackle the associated thought patterns, there's a risk that these bad habits will become engrained, making your child potentially vulnerable to depressive illness later in life.

Feeling Blue, Thinking Blue

The previous chapter introduced a cognitive behavioral model that stresses the way in which thoughts, feelings, behavior, and physical sensations are all connected and influence each other. Researchers have discovered that depressed people, and those vulnerable to depression, demonstrate a characteristic style of thinking. Not surprisingly, if you consistently think like a depressed person, chances are, you will become depressed. The same is true for those who suffer from chronic anxiety.

Martin Seligman has highlighted distinctive differences in the way depressed and nondepressed people explain the things that happen to them. The following example will hopefully illustrate these crucial differences so that you can become more aware of patterns to challenge in your own child's thinking and beneficial habits that can be useful to encourage.

Aaron is 12 years old. He has recently joined a local swim team, and there's a competition this weekend. He desperately wants to be selected, but when the coach announces the team at the next practice, Aaron's name isn't on the list. He feels crushed and sick with disappointment. Seeing how upset he is, his father asks him what's wrong. Aaron shouts at his dad that he "doesn't want to talk about it" and storms off to his room. When he has calmed down sufficiently, he finally offers the following explanation:

Aaron: I don't know why I even joined the stupid swim team. I will never be any good. Lots of people are better than me. I should have gotten the message after last Thursday: My times are too slow. Mr. Jackson obviously thinks I'm a complete loser. Maybe I just don't have any talent after all. I wanted to do this so badly. Why doesn't anything ever work out for me, Dad? It's just not fair....

Father: Hold on a minute ... didn't you tell me that you came in third in the breaststroke heats on Thursday?

Aaron: Yeah, but that was just a fluke, and I wasn't able to keep it up in the other races. Dennis said there had been some bug going around, so I probably only did alright because the others weren't fully better. Anyway, I didn't get picked: I'm just garbage. I'd better just get used to it.

When we look closer at Aaron's comments, we find all the hallmarks of a classically depressive style of thinking. Look at the way Aaron positions himself in regard to this disappointing turn of events. First, he doesn't see his failure to be selected as a temporary setback; he sees it as a permanent obstacle to his *ever* being on the team. He concludes that he will "*never* be any good" and blames factors such as an innate lack of talent that are enduring and unchangeable.

This is typical of the way depressed people think. When bad things happen, they tend to see them as indicative of a *permanent* state, whereas nondepressive people are much more inclined to see the problem as a temporary one. More optimistic people are psychologically more open to reversals of their bad fortune in future, whereas depressives are disposed to think that only good situations will not last.

> Be aware of signs of depressed thinking—that all things are bad and will stay bad, that nothing ever works or is any good, and that this is "always happening to me."
>
>

Second, Aaron explains his failure to make the team in *global* terms rather than factors specific to a particular context. A nondepressed thinking style might have produced explanations that highlight exceptional circumstances: Perhaps the coach felt that putting a new member of the group on the team at such an early stage might have given Aaron too much pressure. Maybe the team for that particular competition had been selected before Aaron joined.

Aaron, however, automatically regards his plight as a reflection of a universal principle that "nothing" ever works out for him. He sees his failure to make the team as further evidence of what an unfair place the world in general is proving to be. He has not just failed to make the team for one race meeting; in his head, he is now a "loser," a position that has wider ramifications. From his despondent vantage point, Aaron can see nothing but further disappointment ahead in all walks of life.

Third, when bad things happen to depressive people, they tend to blame *internal* qualities in themselves rather than external aspects of the situation. In Aaron's mind, the outcome of the selection process is due to the "fact" that he is "garbage" and evidently viewed as such by the coach. As far as Aaron is concerned, he has not been selected because he is inferior to the other swimmers. His lack of talent (a fixed, person-centered explanation) means that he might as well give up.

Aaron doesn't ask himself whether the explanation for the bad event might have nothing to do with him or might be due to factors beyond his control, as a nondepressive thinker would. He doesn't stop to consider that the coach might not have noticed his outstanding performance in the breaststroke trials, or that there might be factors shaping the selection process that he is unaware of. For Aaron, this is a personal failure for which he must take sole responsibility.

Interestingly, when his father attempts to offer him some consolation by reminding him of his breaststroke performance, Aaron reverses his strategy. This *good* event is not seen as due to any skill or ability on his part: It was "a fluke." Unlike his failure, Aaron sees his success as temporary and, as an exception to the rule, has no broader implications of any value. Other people's performance must have been influenced by illness. Aaron brushes aside evidence that doesn't fit with his bleak vision of himself and the world.

A Different Perspective

Sally joined the swim team the same time as Aaron. Like Aaron, Sally also was not picked to be on the team. And like Aaron, she also felt initially disappointed. However, the sense that she makes of the situation is very different. Witness the conversation that she has with her mother the same evening.

Mother: Are you okay, Sally? You're pretty quiet this evening.

Sally: I'm just really ticked off. I didn't get picked for the swim team on Saturday.

Mother: Oh, I'm sorry to hear that.

Sally: Well, I suppose it doesn't matter too much. There are lots of other competitions coming up this season. If I train hard, I'm sure I can still make the team. Maybe Mr. Jackson didn't want to take a risk with me this time around. It's a very important meet for the club. He didn't pick that new boy, Aaron, either, and he got a really fast time in the breaststroke trials on Thursday. Maybe he wants to play it safe for now.

Mother: But you're really good at swimming. I don't understand.

Sally: I suppose I just have to prove that to Mr. Jackson. Last Thursday I did have a bit of an off day and my back was still sore after gym on Wednesday, so I wasn't at my best last week. Maybe I should let him see that medal I won at school. I just need to show him what I can do. There's plenty of time before the end of the season.

Sally's outlook is obviously much more upbeat, but closer analysis also reveals a very different "attributional style." Unlike Aaron, Sally doesn't blame herself; she looks around for exceptional *situational* factors that might explain the coach's decision. She sees the decision as a *temporary* setback that she can reverse by training harder and drawing Mr. Jackson's attention to herself. She doesn't dismiss her failure to qualify as indicative of a lack of talent, but sees it as the result of having "an off day." Moreover, unlike Aaron, Sally doesn't believe that her current exclusion from the team has any broader implications for her performance, either as a swimmer or in any other area of her life. She keeps the significance of her failure tightly contained and *localized.*

It's not difficult to appreciate how, when repeated and ingrained over time, such contrasting explanatory styles can have a profound impact on a child's mood and mental robustness. Children who habitually think like Sally have been proven to have a much greater resilience to depression, whereas the Aarons of this world are likely to join the 10 percent of us who experience clinical depression at some point in their lives. So as a concerned parent, how can you help?

Supporting Healthy Thinking

You can help your child develop a nondepressive stance by making both of you conscious of the way your child is interpreting what is happening to her. If your child is not too down in the dumps, you can use the three dimensions we've just outlined to ask pertinent questions that will encourage her to view things differently. You can also challenge the key dimensions of unduly pessimistic styles of thinking directly:

Response	Functions
"Aaron, I understand how disappointed you feel at the moment, but you're talking as if not qualifying for this one competition means that you will never be on the team. What makes you think that?"	• Acknowledges the emotional reality of the situation • Challenges the perceived *permanence* of the bad event • Invites a more objective review of available evidence
"I am totally confident that if you train hard, you will have faster and faster times. But even if you never get picked, that doesn't make you a 'loser' or a 'garbage' person. Do you choose your friends on the basis of what they can do? Maybe you and I need to do some thinking about what makes someone valuable...."	• Challenges the *generalized significance* of the bad event • Disputes the underlying core assumption: "I am worthless" • Introduces a new frame of reference and gives an invitation to think more flexibly
"You're being really hard on yourself, Aaron. Maybe the reason has nothing to do with you. Let's see whether we can think of any other reasons why Mr. Jackson might not have picked you on this occasion...."	• Challenges a *self-focused* explanation of the bad event • Explores other alternatives • Invites a rational appraisal to counter the emotional, knee-jerk reaction

Help your child think positively and optimistically, with a balanced outlook. Teach constructive responses to bad events.

As always, try to lead by example. Children absorb and often imitate the way the adults around him react. The years we spend as parents can be a hard, demanding period of our lives when our responsibilities can weigh heavily upon us and we enjoy less personal freedom. However rewarding we find our role as parents, most of us struggle at times. Under pressure, it's all too easy to take things personally, lose perspective, and feel that life has it in for us. Nevertheless, our influence means that we need to keep an eye on our reactions and interpretations. Relatively subtle differences in approach can set powerful precedents for children that can shape their thinking styles for years to come.

Check how *you* are interpreting events—make sure you aren't teaching them bad habits by accident. If you realize you've made a mistake, point it out and say why. •

Foster a family culture in which everyone, regardless of age, is invited to share responsibility for promoting the well-being of other family members. When they are old enough to understand these principles, give your children permission to challenge you when they spot an unhelpful attitude or negative way of thinking.

When you get it wrong (as we all do at times), don't hesitate to point out your own mistakes. For some children, it is far easier to learn from your errors than from their own. You are also making the important point that developing and maintaining good emotional and mental discipline is the labor of a lifetime. Constructive thinking habits are something we all have to work at.

Masters of Their Universe

One of the striking features of Sally's narrative is that she sees herself as capable of remedying her situation by applying herself in future training sessions, whereas Aaron displays the characteristic "learned helplessness" of a depressive personality.

Depressed people typically experience themselves as having very little control over their lives, and there is an important overlap between these two states. To be depressed is, on one level, to feel out of control. This is probably why the behavior of depressed boys, in particular, can so often resemble that of thwarted toddlers. When thinking about children's vulnerability to depression, it is probably important to recognize that being a child is a condition that involves more than its fair share of powerlessness.

Early childhood, especially, is a period of our lives when we have virtually no say about what happens to us. Most decisions are made on our behalf by our parents. Things happen to us that we do not want and that we would not choose. We are put into clothes that sometimes don't feel comfortable, have food pushed into our mouths that we don't like, and find ourselves carted into a wide variety of situations at the whim of our caregivers.

For quite a long period, we don't even enjoy control over our most basic bodily functions. This may be why, for toddlers, continence can often become such a political issue. It can be a proud assertion of self-control or a weapon against the authority of others. In infancy, we can do virtually nothing for ourselves. For all practical purposes, we are completely helpless.

In infancy, our helplessness is so extreme that, I suspect, most of the time (uncomfortable wet diapers and empty stomachs aside), it's probably scarcely an issue. When toddlers start to taste the possibility of control, the true extent of their relative powerlessness begins to sink in. This is often when the battles between parents and their offspring really begin. The "terrible twos" is a rather optimistic euphemism for a campaign that often extends far beyond the third year of life—depending, of course, on the temperament of your child.

We all need to feel some degree of control over our lives. Rats put in an experimental condition in which electric shocks were administered to them in a random, unpredictable fashion soon become listless and make no efforts to safeguard themselves. They appear to "give up," behaving just like depressed people. Conversely, when seeing clinically depressed patients, one of the first steps many therapists take is to get their clients involved in "activity scheduling." This involves negotiating small, manageable goals that, over time, allow clients to recover some sense of themselves as effective, capable people who are not completely powerless.

Giving your children opportunities to master situations and use their talents isn't just about making them into more rounded individuals: It is also an important protective measure against future mental health problems. Young children quite rightly take great pride in their accomplishments, and caregivers should create conditions in which children can experience the satisfactions of successfully completing challenges and acting more independently.

Give your child some areas of control in her life. Allow him to make some choices—just not over everything.

Of course, a balance must be struck. For a child, having too much power can be just as stressful as having too little. Much has been written about the psychological difficulties of living in a modern world that overwhelms us with so many opportunities and choices on a daily basis. Children need to feel contained. They appear to sense that they are not yet equipped to manage themselves or their lives independent of their caregivers. Consequently, a child who has been given too much control within the family is seldom a happy one. A key skill of parenting is the ability to navigate this perilous border. This means encouraging a child's sense of autonomy without undermining her security—and the latter depends upon the child's perception that someone loving and competent is ultimately running the show.

Research suggests that it's a good idea to encourage your child to make choices, develop competencies, and function independently, but always within sensible parameters. If you give your preschool child *carte blanche* choice over what he wants to wear every day, get ready to head to the supermarket each week in the company of an increasingly grubby Spiderman or Wonder Woman. And if you do create this expectation, prepare yourself for a royal battle when the day comes you do need him to wear something warmer or (in your view) more appropriate at your parents' golden wedding celebration.

On the other hand, giving a young child regular experience of more restricted either/or choices ("Do you want to wear your *red* shirt today, Callum, or the *blue* one?") fosters a sense of control at a level that will likely prove acceptable to you and helpful for your child. Obviously, as your child grows toward the teenage years, he will be able to take on a more significant level of control and personal responsibility, but the expansion needs to be gradual. Teenagers who are suddenly given a large measure of personal freedom without adequate preparation in earlier childhood can easily feel overwhelmed and are highly vulnerable to peer pressure.

As your child gets older, gradually increase the amount of control she has over her own life, making a gradual transition from toddlers' simple choices to late teenage independence.

As your child gets older, resist the temptation to keep your baby dependent on you. Teach the skills that will ultimately help him function in life and view himself as a competent individual. You can enhance a child's sense of mastery enormously by teaching practical skills: how to cook, how to read a map, how to balance a bank account. Does your teenager know how to resuscitate someone, wire an electrical plug, or do his own ironing? We need to help our children develop a sure sense of themselves as capable individuals who can handle whatever life throws at them.

It's a great shame that many teenagers leave for college still unable to fend for themselves or even perform simple domestic tasks. Don't let your child join their ranks. If we allow our offspring to become passive and helpless, we are also predisposing them toward a depressive mindset.

Giving Them a Leg Up

To help children develop their sense of mastery, parents need to operate sensitively in what the Russian psychologist Lev Vygotsky called "the zone of proximal development." This might sound like something out of a sci-fi movie, but the concept is a simple one. Vygotsky believed that children learn best when given appropriate support to help them accomplish tasks that lie just beyond their unaided reach. By helping to structure the task, or by directing the child's attention to relevant aspects of it, an adult can often help a child reach the next level of ability. By gradually internalizing such "scaffolding" experiences, children become more capable of performing similar tasks on their own.

For scaffolding to work effectively, it is vital that the caregiver assist the child without "taking over" or rushing ahead. Asking pertinent questions that will enable the child to find his own solutions is far more helpful to your child than giving him the answers yourself. Drawing comparisons between aspects of the current task and relevant skills already in your child's repertoire can also be a productive strategy. Simply providing an interested commentary describing what you see your child doing can foster a level of self-awareness that can pave the way for a breakthrough.

In scaffolding, your role is to act as a resource and support rather than a teacher. Make occasional suggestions, by all means, if you sense that your child is becoming disheartened and frustrated, but resist the temptation to do too much. If your child can successfully find her own way through a challenging task, the rewards will be much sweeter and the resultant sense of achievement much greater.

Give children tasks to do that are just out of their reach unaided but that are possible with a little bit of guidance or advice: "If you color in the petals, I'll help you do the leaves...."

"Praise You Like I Should..."

When pitched appropriately, the right kind of praise can really help develop your child's sense of competence. When you praise your child, try to avoid generalizations and focus on the specifics. Instead of simply enthusing about "what a lovely painting" your child has done, pick out aspects of it that you feel are worthy of special mention:

> "I really like the way you've used all the different colors to create the sense of light coming through the leaves."

> "It's terrific how these figures here really look as if they're running across the park. How did you manage to make them look as if they're moving?"

> "The amount of detail in your picture makes it really interesting to look at … there's so much going on here, Robert—it's amazing!"

These kinds of observations not only let your child know that you are genuinely appreciative of the product, but also provide feedback that will help build and develop skills.

Discriminating praise is ultimately much more valuable to your child than pretending that everything he or she does is wonderful. There is a common misconception that constantly affirming children through praise is the royal road to self-esteem. However, Positive Psychology research stresses that a far more reliable foundation of self-esteem is the individual's personal experience of succeeding and mastering challenges, both great and small, throughout the course of life. To accomplish this, your child needs honest, constructive feedback, as well as your affirmation and encouragement.

> Give detailed feedback and constructive criticism rather than
> blanket praise.
>
>

Individuals who view themselves as competent and able to achieve their goals are more likely to feel good about themselves and be psychologically robust. Always let your child know that your love for her is unconditional. However, if your praise is too fulsome and always couched in generalities, it likely will rapidly become a devalued currency for your children.

When you do offer praise, keep the emphasis also on the personal qualities that your child has shown or the skills he has employed rather than just the outcome of his labors. You want to reinforce the attitudes and approaches that will enhance your child's ability to achieve future goals:

> "I'm really impressed with how you have managed to stick with that math homework, even thought I know you felt like giving up. But you got through it, and now you won't have it hanging over you this weekend."

> "You've gotten so much more organized in the way you're approaching things these days, Charlie. I noticed how you laid out all the ingredients before you started making the cake—which, by the way, is incredibly light and moist...."

> "That five minutes you put into brainstorming ideas beforehand really paid off. Your story is so imaginative. By the end, I really wanted to know how it was going to work out."

Attending to the process rather than just the outcome of their efforts also helps children derive value from their sense of themselves as learners who are constantly expanding and developing their skills base. This stops them from seeing themselves as people whose worth depends solely on what they can achieve.

Finally, as your child develops a taste for mastery, she will learn to place greater value on the mental skills and attitudes needed to expand it. Very few worthwhile challenges can be successfully accomplished without tolerating frustration, subduing impulses, and delaying immediate gratification. As you give a child opportunities to control the world around her, you are also reinforcing the rewards of controlling herself and helping her practice these essential skills.

We have already noted that the parts of the brain involved in planning, coordinating, and focusing activity are precisely the same regions that are involved in regulating emotions. Exercising this mental muscle in a context in which the rewards are so motivating has the added benefit of making your child more able to manage turbulence in his emotional life. This, in turn, should give him greater control over his behavior.

Promoting Mindfulness

One the most exciting recent developments in the modern treatment of depression has been the integration of cognitive behavioral principles with insights from an Eastern tradition that goes back many thousands of years.

The practice of mindfulness is a form of meditation that emphasizes closing down depressive thinking by paying attention only to the present moment and accepting the contents of your thoughts. Instead of striving to change the contents of your thoughts overtly, practitioners of the mindfulness approach develop the capacity to "bear witness" to them in a relaxed, nonjudgmental fashion. Those who develop this discipline are often able to break the stranglehold of the depressed state of mind.

Psychologists have sought to understand why the mindfulness approach can be so effective. They believe that one of the main drivers of a depressive mindset is obsessive "discrepancy analysis"—in other words, a preoccupation with the seemingly insurmountable gap between where you are and where you would like to be. Their suggestion is that the mindfulness approach short-circuits this painful and counterproductive process of comparison by not attempting to change the present or look beyond it, but to accept it for what it is, even if it is distressing or unpleasant.

The reality is that our experience changes moment by moment, but, as we have already seen, a depressed person usually ignores or edits out anything that might prove neutral or even uplifting. The practice of mindfulness keeps the individual open to experience in a way that runs counter to the habits of a depressed mind. It stops people from getting caught up in cycles of negative thinking by holding everything lightly and helping people become observers of their own thoughts rather than their slaves.

Research evidence shows that the practice of mindfulness really can help reduce relapse among depressed adults, and the key attitudes also likely underpin a mentally healthy outlook.

We can certainly encourage our children to develop some of the hallmarks of mindfulness. Learning to concentrate, to really observe, and to live in the present is a talent that has to be developed. It starts with learning to still the babbling of busy young minds and bring attention back to the job at hand. The modern world leaves us in a constantly overstimulated state: We are awash with a barrage of information from the media and the Internet; our lives consist of constantly changing priorities and roles.

> Encourage your child to concentrate, ignore distractions, really observe, and live in the present.

Because we've gotten used to dealing with constant flux and so many competing demands, the simplicity and focus of doing one thing at a time is becoming quite alien to us. If the level of stimulation drops below the cultural norm, many children feel ill at ease. Teach your child to be as comfortable with simplicity and silence as she is with the pyrotechnics of the multimedia age.

No one is designed to multitask all the time. How is your child to learn to attend to the flavors and textures of food if every meal is accompanied by the distraction of the TV set? Take your child out into nature and train him to observe: Point out details and examine the intricate veins on the back of a leaf, the ridges on shells, or the glistening trails left by the snails. Stand on a hillside together; close your eyes together and see whether you can concentrate on listening—really listening— for a whole minute. Start doing these things while your child is young, and you will be encouraging good mental hygiene in later life.

Take your child outside and let her study the tiniest details of nature. Help her learn to be comfortable with simplicity and silence.

It's a shame that the art of collecting things is becoming so neglected. Whether it's stamps, beer mats, or bottle caps, poring over a prized collection trains children to focus their attention in a way not encouraged by the fast-moving world of videos and computer games.

I'm sounding like an old fogey, but I make no apology. The latest health research is telling us that the ability to live fully in the moment and develop a quality of sustained attention has genuine protective value for all of us.

The 17th -century French moralist Jean de la Bruyère claimed that "children have neither past nor future; they enjoy the present." However, although children might have an innate talent for "living in the moment," we need to remember that life has changed, making it difficult to hang on to this valuable ability. If we are serious about protecting our children's mental health, we may need to work a little harder if we want our children to be able to swim upstream against the constant distractions of modern life.

Quick Summary
Action Points

- Depressed states of mind are often responsible for bad behavior in children.

- Learn to spot and challenge characteristic features of a depressed mindset:

  → Bad events interpreted as permanent, far-reaching, and person-related

  → Good events regarded as temporary, localized, and a product of external factors

- Nurture your child's sense of mastery to ward off "learned helplessness":

  → Provide opportunities to meet challenges and develop practical skills.

  → Offer a young child controlled choices—for example, by using either/or alternatives.

  → Develop your child's sense of control through effective scaffolding.

- Use discriminating praise:

  → Be specific about the merits of what your child has done.

  → Focus on the process as well as the product: Affirm attitudes, qualities, and strategies that will ensure future success.

- Help your child develop a "mindful" approach toward life:

    → Create periods at home when distractions are kept to a minimum.

    → Avoid constant multitasking and help your child learn to pay attention to detail.

    → Foster a taste for stillness and simplicity.

FIVE

Wrestling with Monsters: Overcoming Stress and Anxiety

"Sometimes I just lie there and so many things are in my mind I find it really hard to get to sleep. You know when a plane lands at night and you look out of the window and you see this big spider's web of twinkling lights? Well, that's what it's like in my head. Each of those little lights is a different worry. ... If I zoom in on one of them, it's like when the plane gets close to the ground and you can only see a few of the lights at a time—but the rest are still out there somewhere. When you are that close up, you can't see the others anymore. But they're still there."
—James, 10 years old

We can all be seduced by a vision of childhood as an endless summer of carefree, cloudless skies and dreamless nights. Perhaps this is because we so badly want it to be like this for our own kids. Or maybe we need to believe that there is an alternative to the demanding, cynical world we often inhabit as adults. Whatever the reason, we cannot afford to pretend that our children are growing up in a protected bubble. These days, children have to cope with many of the same pressures of modern life as the rest of us. And just like us, sometimes they struggle. Unfortunately, when children aren't coping well with the stress in their lives, it can have a dramatic impact on their behavior.

Understanding what causes stress in children, and giving them tools to deal with anxiety, is one of the most valuable investments parents can make in their future well-being. Managing stress is one of the fundamental skills upon which children's ability to regulate their behavior depends.

How Stress Affects Us

Stress and aggression go hand in hand. As we all know from school biology lessons, when our backs are against the wall, our minds and bodies prepare us to do one of two things: run away, or come out fighting. This is a mechanism that has served our species well since prehistoric times. It prevented our ancestors from ending up as *hors d'oeuvres* for all manner of scary Jurassic predators. However, it also means that under stress, people of all ages are primed to attack. The "cooling" mechanisms that usually restrain antisocial behavior have less influence because, in crisis mode, we are programmed to give priority to the rapid-response survival circuits of the primitive brain. The brakes are off.

We can all recognize how much more easily we are provoked when stressed. As adults, even low-level background stress can leave us cranky, irritable, and prone to snapping at friends, family, and colleagues. Under acute stress, some people become physically violent. In rare circumstances, extreme stress can cause reasonable people to act in completely irrational ways that have devastating consequences.

If such things can happen to adults, with their fully developed frontal lobes and years of self-restraint practice, how much more vulnerable are children to the effects of anxiety on their behavior? Before shaking our heads in despair at the public display of antisocial behavior, perhaps we should pause to consider the role chronic stress plays in both the extremes of antisocial behavior and the more commonplace tantrums of our own little angels.

Natural-Born Stressheads?

Susceptibility to stress varies enormously between children. Over recent years, much work has been done to map personality research to the physiology and biology of the brain.

Of all the aspects of personality that have been used to measure differences among people, the trait of neuroticism has proven one of the most reliable. It has taken its rightful place among the "Big Five," the key dimensions of personality in which researchers now have the most confidence. People who score highly on neuroticism are born worriers. As Woody Allen once remarked, "I am not afraid to die; I just don't want to be there when it happens." Neurotic individuals are, by definition, highly vulnerable to stress.

Psychologist Daniel Nettle suggests that the features associated with neuroticism can best be summarized by heightened sensitivity to negative feelings of all kinds. This is supported by the fact that people who suffer from full-blown anxiety disorders such as phobias, obsessive compulsive disorder, and post-traumatic stress are more likely to score highly on this trait.

We are beginning to achieve a better understanding of the biology behind these tendencies. For instance, the amygdala (seat of the primitive emotion-driven brain) seems to be more active and even bigger and denser in people who score highly on neuroticism measures. Physical differences also show up in their prefrontal cortex—in precisely the area that usually lights up on scan when people need to suppress negative reactions.

Klaus-PeterLesch has discovered that people who score high on neuroticism are also more likely to be carrying a short form of a piece of genetic code known as the serotonin transporter gene. Because this is the neurotransmitter most closely identified with soothing anxious and depressed states of mind, serotonin plays a key role in Mother Nature's technology for "kissing to make it better." Drugs such as Prozac are thought to work (although who knows these days?) by preventing the body from reabsorbing serotonin. The calming effects of physical exercise are also probably related to their effect on the brain's serotonergic pathways. The good news for many of us, is that chocolate also affects the nervous system in much the same way. It's a hard call.

Such findings suggest that some people are naturally biased toward neuroticism and the high levels of anxiety that go with it. If your child is among them, the advice in this chapter is especially relevant. However, even the most mellow of us has our limits, and no child is immune to the eroding effects that stress can have on reasonable behavior.

The Hallmarks of a Stressed Child

"I swear he's possessed," complained the mother of six-year-old Harry. "He has been in a foul mood for most of the week, and yesterday I found him in his sister's room cheerfully disemboweling her toy cat with a kitchen knife. The stuffing was flying everywhere. But the moment I went into the room, he looked up at me with these big helpless eyes (the knife still in his hand, mind you) and yelled, 'It wasn't me!' Then suddenly his face crumpled up and he started howling. His father keeps asking when his period's due!"

What Harry's mother was describing is fairly typical of a child under duress, and it was no great surprise to discover that Harry's behavior was most likely a delayed reaction to a recent move of the family to a new house. Abrupt mood swings, lying, and bullying behavior can all be the outward signs of internal pressure as your child's powers of self-control break down. For the reasons already mentioned, stressed children might also report finding it difficult to concentrate and can become more forgetful than usual.

When stress hormone levels are elevated, they can also produce some of the physical symptoms of anxiety: feeling out of breath, shaky, or dizzy. Your child may appear to be "coming down with something," complaining of pins and needles, headaches, stomach cramps, or a sudden feeling of hot or cold. Increased sweating might leave the skin clammy to the touch, and the psychological effects of these hormones can make your child feel unsettled and strange. Sleep patterns can also be disrupted, and your child may start having nightmares—even if the content of these appears to be unrelated to anything going on in your child's everyday life.

If your child is ever unfortunate enough to suffer a full-blown panic attack, these symptoms might increase in intensity to the point that both you and your child fear that there is something seriously physically wrong. In the throes of a panic attack, people can suffer from palpitations, a loss of feeling in their limbs, choking sensations, and disorientation. They experience intense fear that they are going mad or even about to die. In fact, although panic attacks are acutely disturbing when they occur, their symptoms are physically harmless. However, if things are this bad, your child may require professional help and you should talk to your family doctor.

As far as anxiety responses within the "normal" range are concerned, you should also be on the lookout for signs of regressive behavior. Anxious children might turn back the clock emotionally by resorting to habits and long-outgrown patterns of behavior, such as sucking their thumb or wanting to keep you in sight at all times. Older children are more likely to become defiant, objectionable, surly, rude, and withdrawn.

Before we look at some techniques your child can use to combat anxious thinking, it is worth becoming aware of the sorts of things that cause children to become stressed. Although they overlap with adult concerns, some of them are specific to children and might not even be immediately obvious to our adult eyes.

Is the News Bad News for Children?

Many children get very concerned about current affairs. In moderation, television can be a great source of education and entertainment for kids. But unrestricted viewing also confronts children with realities many of them are not psychologically ready to digest: They will witness scenes of violence and blood-shed, see starving and abandoned children from all over the world, and hear reports of children being abducted from hotel rooms while they sleep.

Listen to the questions children ask, and you will be left in little doubt about the undercurrent of anxiety that exposure to the media can stir up: "Can our house flood like those ones on the news?" "If there was a war in our country, would you have to go and fight, Daddy?" "What will happen to Pez [the family dog] when the sun burns up the Earth?" "When will I get cancer like that girl with no hair?"

In the mid-1990s, I was a junior researcher in a government-funded study that followed a group of children from infancy into their teenage years. Part of my job was to interview them and their parents about various aspects of their lives. The children were eight years old when I went to see them, but I distinctly remember being constantly surprised by how many parents said their children had nightmares about current affairs stories they had heard on the news or seen on TV.

It's all too easy to leave the television on in the background—we may not even be conscious of what our children are taking in. Unfortunately, children often lack the information, experience, or understanding to put news stories into context or assess risks realistically. Because of this, children tend to fill in the gaps with their imagination. An eye-catching headline can provide the seed for vivid nightmare scenarios that can later keep them awake at night.

If you are going to allow your child to watch the news, I recommend that until your child reaches age ten, you restrict viewing to current affairs programs aimed at a younger audience. Also, it can be helpful to make this an activity in which you and your child sit down and watch together. First, you will know exactly what he has seen. More important, you will be able to review the content of the program with him. In this way, you have an opportunity to tackle any fears and offer a more balanced perspective.

Don't be afraid to ask younger children directly whether they have concerns about anything they have seen on the screen so you know how to respond. You will also be encouraging a family culture in which your child gets used to voicing his fears. This is particularly important in light of a recent Kidscape survey reporting that only a quarter of 9 to 13 year olds were prepared to share their worries with a parent.

If you let your child who's under ten watch the news, be there with her and ask if anything she has seen bothers her.

If your child does confide a fear about something she has seen or heard, always take it seriously. Resist the temptation to laugh it off or dismiss it out of hand. This won't make your child feel any better. Children can get anxious about things that might seem absurd to grown-ups, but if they feel ridiculed, they may well decide to keep their concerns to themselves in the future. Many of our own fears are irrational, but that doesn't make them any less real. Giving your child's anxieties thoughtful consideration and adopting a pragmatic, problem-solving approach is helpful on a number of levels. Not only does it demonstrate that you are engaging with your child's concerns, but it also shows that a rational, reasoned response can go a long way to setting her mind at ease.

Never laugh off a child's anxiety, however silly it may seem to you. Always give a thoughtful, rational response.

Schoolwork Stress

In my clinical work, I come across more and more children who are severely stressed about how they are doing at school, and these children are just the tip of the iceberg. Recent surveys confirm that academic performance is a pressing source of concern for many children. For many children, fears about not doing well at school are often linked to anxieties about their future prospects after they leave. As one perfectly able eight-year-old confided to me through floods of tears, "I am not the brightest in the class ... I'm bound to get a *really* bad job." That children as young as this boy should be thinking this way is terribly sad, but as parents, we need to recognize that the pressure children experience in this area feels very real. Right or wrong, a surprising number of children are convinced that, without the right qualifications, they stand little chance of achieving a secure foothold upon an uncertain future.

Of course, many parents share this belief and the anxiety that goes with it. Fear is a highly contagious emotion, and it is all too easy for parents and children to infect each other and create a destructive, anxious atmosphere around the whole issue of homework and academic performance.

I am not implying that good grades and qualifications are unimportant or that we shouldn't do everything we can to help our children fulfill their academic potentials. However, we need to hold out against the extreme anxiety-inducing position in many children's minds that *everything* depends upon how well they do at school.

For a start, this is simply not true. Increasingly, evidence suggests that the cluster of nonacademic qualities that make up emotional intelligence is far more likely to determine an individual's long-term prospects. Many of our nation's most successful people left school with very meager qualifications—or none at all.

> Don't let your child believe that success at school is the only thing that matters in life or that a highly paid job is the only aim.
>
>

In any case, we also need to help children challenge the idea that a highly paid job is the only job worth having. Although a powerful advertising industry promotes the idea that acquisition is the key to contentment, all the Positive Psychology research into happiness suggests that an increase in income is correlated with life satisfaction only up to a certain, quite modest level. Beyond that point, it makes no difference. The old saying is true: "Money (well, lots of it, anyway) really cannot buy you happiness." We all want our children to be happy, but we also need to make sure that we are instilling values and priorities that will genuinely promote quality of life.

On a purely practical level, if we put children under too much pressure to succeed, we actually make it harder for them to do their best. Psychologists have known for a long time that chronic stress makes it harder to think and concentrate. Rather unfairly, if you are already feeling under pressure at school, this side effect will likely make life even more stressful for you, especially in a classroom setting. We are now beginning to understand a little more about the way stress affects the brain.

Cortisol is one of the main stress hormones. It is designed to shock the body into battle readiness, and it does a very efficient job. But in a threatening situation in which there is no appropriate fight-or-flight response to neutralize cortisol levels, this hormone stays in the blood stream longer than it should.

The hippocampus is an area of the brain that plays a key role in memory and the coordination of information, and it appears to be particularly sensitive to the effects of stress hormones. In some people with chronically elevated cortisol levels, signs of physical damage even show up on scans. One study found that the hippocampus in brains of adult Vietnamese subjects suffering from post-traumatic stress disorder (a condition that bathes the brain in cortisol over long periods) appeared to have shrunk by up to 8%. The impact that stress can have on the developing brains of children is not yet fully understood, but findings such as these do not bode well.

Of course, not all stress is bad for you or your child. Children need to be put into situations that challenge, excite, and extend them. Occasional, controlled exposure to stress can improve their performance in some settings. However, generally high stress levels are not helpful and can significantly undermine children's performance at school.

Continual assessment means that many children (and their parents) experience the sustained pressure of trying to achieve high marks for every piece of graded course work. Stress in a more acute form comes from formal tests and exams, when younger children can also become very stressed. However sensitively they are administered, children are fully aware that their ability is being measured, and for some of them, this is highly anxiety-provoking. Sadly, children have a tendency to believe that it is not just their reading age or math skills that are being graded, but their worth as people.

For dealing with anxieties about school performance, many of the techniques for dealing with anxious thoughts (covered later in this chapter) are relevant. However, parents might find the following suggestions helpful:

> ➤ Try to stay relaxed yourself. Remember that children develop at different rates, especially in the early years. However, if you are worried about your child's performance at school, be proactive: Make an appointment to discuss your concerns with the relevant teacher who will be able to give you accurate feedback and make suggestions for how you can best support your child's learning.

> ➤ Keep the channels of communication with your child open. Be sensitive to periods during which he might feel under pressure, and give him opportunities to talk about his fears. However, also respect the fact that a stressed child might not always want to talk; at times like these, find practical ways to remind him of your love and support. Home baking always worked for me.

> ➤ If your child is overly anxious about performance, work through her catastrophic beliefs about the

implications of not doing well at school. Help her challenge negative thoughts that her worth as a person or future prospects hinge entirely or her grades, or that a low mark on a math test means that she will be living in a shop doorway later in life.

➤ Don't make your approval dependent upon achievement. By all means, express pride in your child's accomplishments, but focus your praise on the qualities and attitudes that helped him do well: his dedication, his focus, his hard work. Always emphasize the importance of fulfilling personal potential over being the best. Sooner or later, your child will meet someone brighter, faster, and more able.

➤ Make an effort to affirm the value of your child's achievements outside of school work. Celebrate his skill on the football field, her soccer skills, his comic timing, the fact that your neighbors now consider her responsible enough to baby-sit for them.

➤ Teach your child to see "failure" or low grades as useful feedback and part of an ongoing learning process that will help him develop. Cultivate what Carol Dweck calls a "growth mindset" in which all setbacks are viewed as learning opportunities. Emphasize that ability is not fixed, but can always be developed through practice.

➤ Concentrate on developing skills that will enable your child to feel more in control of her own learning. For more information on these "metaskills," see Chapter 7, "Unstoppable: Boosting Your Child's Problem-Solving Skills." Also help your child organize her schoolwork efficiently so that she can protect periods of free time during which she can relax and "switch off" from the demands of school.

Taking It Personally

"WHAT'S **WRONG** WITH YOU?!? JUST STOP NAGGING AT ME, YOU BITCH!" screams 11-year-old Jason, slamming the door on his bemused mother, who has innocently suggested that he should think about getting his hair cut if he wants it to stop flopping in his eyes.

Furious at overhearing his father informing a family friend that he has been feeling "a bit poorly" that morning, four-year-old Duncan suddenly howls in protest, "I FEEL **MORE** THAN A LIT-TLE BIT POORLY!" His trembling indignation is palpable.

Looking at these examples, you might well be wondering, what on earth is going on here? Jason certainly crossed a line in speaking so abusively toward his mother, but the real question is, why did these two boys react so strongly to such innocuous remarks?

The answer probably has something to do with a source of tension in childhood that often lies well hidden beneath the surface: namely, the underlying fragility of many children's sense of self.

"Hold on a minute," you object. "This doesn't sound like the voice of self-doubt to me. Surely, what the Jasons and Duncans of this world need is to be taken down a peg or two." I agree that Jason's abusive comments are unacceptable and demand a robust response. However, if we ignore the psychological dynamics driving this kind of behavior, we could end up targeting the symptom rather than the cause.

The term *primary narcissism* refers to a perfectly normal phase of development. It describes periods when children can become especially self-centered, demanding, and completely unable to tolerate things being other than precisely the way they want them. You often see it most prominently in toddlers, but it can re-emerge once more during the teenage years. Narcissists, whether young or old, can be pretty tiresome company. Prickly if criticized, they carry around with them a dramatically inflated sense of their importance in the scheme of things. However obnoxious, what needs to be recognized is that underneath all the bravado and arrogance, the narcissist is overcompensating for a gnawing insecurity.

Deep down, all narcissists are trying to protect themselves from feelings of shame. They question the ability of the world to meet their needs, and much of their energy is devoted to monitoring and protecting their brittle identities. Being constantly on the defensive like this is inevitably stressful and makes narcissistic people of all ages hypersensitive to criticism. Even constructive feedback or the most innocent of suggestions can be experienced as a personal assault for a child still feeling his way toward a secure sense of self.

We all anchor our identities by emotionally investing in things. These might include an important relationship; a job; a particular talent; or even possessions, such as a favorite jacket, a CD collection, or, in Jason's case, a particular look or hairstyle. We feel that these things represent us and say something important about who we are. If they are taken from us, we feel diminished. As we get older, we usually become less reliant on these external symbols of self, but children who don't yet know who they are can be highly dependent upon them and feel very threatened if theirs are tampered with. This is partly why so many toddlers find it so hard to share their toys, and why adolescents fight so ferociously with their parents about body piercings, skirt lengths, and tidy bedrooms.

Be aware of things that children have strong emotional attachments to. This includes other people, possessions, or even parts of their body. Any criticism of those things can be devastating to children.

It is important that parents recognize how exposed children can feel during these stages of their development. The background stress generated in their lives is considerable. As the parent, to some extent, you may have to grit your teeth and endure your child's heightened touchiness during such phases. However, there are a few things you can do to make life less stressful for both of you.

> ➤ Where possible, do tread carefully around your child's symbols of self, even if he has made investments that seem trivial or alien to you. Pick your battles wisely.

> ➤ Check that there is a valid reason for asking your child to do what you request. You don't always have to explain yourself, but if your child can manipulate to the point at which you fall back on "Because I say so!" in her own head, she has exposed your nurturing as naked power play. This merely confirms her fears that she needs to be on guard against you in the future.

> ➤ Acknowledge how your child might be feeling—but be careful not to put words into his mouth.

➤ If your child is overly sensitive to criticism, try to use open questions to help her draw her own conclusions about what she might need to learn, to ensure a better outcome in the future.

All Change

For many young children, different equals bad. Remember the last time you washed your child's comforter? Or served up something unfamiliar for lunch? Even such minor alterations are remarkably unsettling for some children.

Whoever devised the saying "A change is as good as a rest" failed to recognize to the mental and emotional demands that change can place on us. Change can indeed revitalize us, but in novel situations in which we can no longer fall back upon established routines, the results can be psychologically taxing. It is no coincidence that the top ten stressors for adults all relate to significant life transitions: the death of a spouse, the end of a relationship, the move to a new house. Even as grown-ups, the amount of change that we can cope with comfortably is limited. It can be great to go on vacation and visit new places, take in new sights and sample a different cuisine, but most of us feel some sense of relief when we step back through our own front door.

Considering how much change children have to manage in the course of their brief lives, it's not surprising that they are wary of it. In the early years, their bodies morph continually, their abilities expand exponentially, and their routines are in a constant state of flux. They have so much to learn and so many skills to acquire that few things in a child's life ultimately remain consistent. Even within their families, more than a third of them will have experienced a separation or divorce by the time they are 16.

Most parents will already be aware of events commonly associated with childhood stress. Death, separation and divorce, the illness of a parent or close relative—such life events can have a powerful effect on some children. However, it is important to recognize that even positive changes can raise stress levels for many kids.

Six-year-old Craig and his mother had recently moved to a new home. Their new home was a spacious apartment that allowed Craig to have his own bedroom for the first time. Craig loved the new apartment and told me proudly about how the walls of his new room had been freshly lined with posters of his football-playing heroes. Nevertheless, he was also confused by how anxious he felt in his new environment. Although it was indisputably better, it just didn't feel the *same* as the old place, with its noisy neighbors and rattling windows.

When told that it was perfectly normal to feel this way and that it might take time to get used to the new apartment, Craig looked enormously relieved. "I just felt bad," he explained. "I didn't want my mom to think I didn't like where we are now, because I *really* do. I just don't quite know myself there yet."

In Craig's case, simply reassuring him that his reaction to change was entirely normal did a lot to ease the pressure he was feeling. If you know your child is facing changes of any kind, whether to do with shifting allegiances within friendship groups or a move to a new school, be aware that he might be more stressed than he acknowledges. On the other hand, if your child's behavior starts falling apart, one of the first questions to ask yourself (and him) is whether anything in his world has altered recently:

> ➤ If you know that a significant change is on the horizon, give your child a chance to prepare. The more information you provide, the more she can picture herself in her new circumstances and get used to the idea. For example, if your child has to go to the hospital for treatment, take her into the ward, arrange for her to meet the staff, and have her talk to someone who has been through the same procedure. Let her ask questions and run through exactly what will happen when she goes in. Instead of feeding anxiety, in most cases, access to knowledge gives children back a sense of control.

> ➤ Present your child with a realistic picture of what will happen. Don't be tempted to gloss over the difficulties or focus exclusively on the benefits.

> ➤ With your child, brainstorm the implications of any big change—positive or negative—in terms of the impact it may have on her life. Draw up a list of pros and cons.

> ➤ Recognize that change often involves an element of loss. Allow your child to experience and express his feelings about it without censoring him. He might need to work through a process of letting go, so give him time.

> ➤ Acknowledge the stress involved in change and understand that most changes in children's lives are orchestrated by other people. Sometimes simply recognizing this can diffuse the tension children feel.

> ➤ If possible, give your child an active role in any changes that affect her. It can be helpful for older siblings to be given responsibilities for looking

143

after a new baby or for an older child to start picking out paint colors for her new room, in anticipation of a house move.

➤ Make clear what will *not* change, and identify any relevant skills that your child is taking with him into the new situation: "I know it isn't the same, Max, but you will still be able to see your friends from your old school on weekends and school breaks. You will no doubt keep chatting with them at all hours on the computer. It can be hard at first in a new school when you don't know anyone yet, but ever since your first day in preschool, I have always been impressed by how good you are at making new friends. Not everyone can do that."

➤ Do give your child opportunities to discuss the change with you and raise any related worries. Sometimes children can get worked up quite needlessly. I know of one child who had assumed that when his family moved to a new town, they would be leaving the cat behind (which was not, in fact, the case). Another child thought that once his much-loved granddad moved into the retirement home, he would no longer be allowed to visit.

Help children prepare for change, however small or large, and anticipate it being difficult for them. Give them the chance to talk over their worries.

144

Too Much Stimulation...
or Too Little?

At wedding receptions, you're likely to find two kinds of children tucked away under the banquet table. The first is usually accompanied by a bright-eyed, giggling cousin as the pair revels in the illicit thrill of stolen champagne or other contraband. For the second, the cool folds of the tablecloth offer a temporary sanctuary from the noise, bustle, and business of the whole occasion.

Psychologists have known for years that different people feel comfortable with different levels of stimulation. Similar to the thermostat on your central heating that turns off the furnace when it gets too hot or fires up the system when the temperature drops below its setting, we all tend to adjust our environment to keep levels of stimulation within the range that suits us.

People who like to keep the stimulation setting high are the extroverts. These are the outgoing, 24-hour party animals whose high-octane lifestyle feeds their need for sensation and excitement. At the other end of the spectrum are the extreme introverts, who are more likely to be found curled up on the sofa with a glass of wine and a good book.

Such differences are hard-wired into the brain and are linked to the way the brain responds to arousal. This doesn't mean that introverts *never* want to let their hair down or that extroverts never stand still. However, the contrasting lifestyles of high-scoring introverts and extroverts is some indication of how driven we are to keep our general level of arousal within the range that suits us.

When we're not able to do this, we become stressed. In fact, the stress response is one of the feedback mechanisms that lets us know we are out of our stimulation comfort zone. Most of us are already aware that overstimulation can have a powerful effect on children. Attend any children's birthday party, and you can witness the results for yourself. For every wild child jumping on your sofa or trying to sling jelly across the room, there will be tear-stained casualties for whom the whole event is proving just too much. However, we are less tuned into the fact that when the stimulation level drops below what we require, this can be equally stressful for us.

Too much or too little stimulation can be bad for children. All children need and want different levels of action and quiet. Get to know your children—and help them get to know themselves.

Boredom is difficult to tolerate, and many children find it unbearable. Most of us recognize that an overstimulated child is likely to have trouble managing behavior, but the same can be said of an understimulated one. One of the first steps that a dog trainer takes with a disobedient or aggressive dog is to make sure that the animal is getting adequate exercise. Understimulated children will resort to desperate measures to get their arousal level back into a more temperate range. You can see this in the way that children strapped into the back of a car for long periods resort to bickering with each other, in an attempt to raise the level of excitement in the immediate environment. Alternatively, they might try to provoke you with a relentless round of "Are we there yet?"–style interrogation.

As your child gets older, it will be useful to help him understand where he lies on the introvert–extrovert scale and what that means in terms of warding off the stress that accompanies too little or too much stimulation. When your child reaches the age of seven, he can take one of the online child-friendly personality tests, such as the Murphy Meisgeier Type Indicator for Children (a children's version of the famous Myers-Briggs test), which will give him some sense of how much stimulation he needs.

Teach your child to recognize when he needs to do something active, interesting, or exciting, and when his internal stress sensors are telling him it's time to take things down a step. Some of the relaxation techniques described in the later section "Self-Soothing Techniques" are useful tools that can enable an overstimulated child to restore his equilibrium.

Alternatively, make sure that your child has a range of suitable activities available so that he can increase stimulation levels when necessary. Ideally, these need to be things that don't always require your involvement or supervision. Many parents end up being blackmailed by their bored children into a constant round of extravagant trips and outings; this is fine once in a while, but it cannot be the staple solution to periods when your child needs to raise his stimulation levels.

Basic sports equipment, such as footballs, jump ropes, and pogo sticks, are ideal for children who crave physical stimulation. Many parents swear that a big garden trampoline is a worthwhile investment for such purposes—and a potentially entertaining one for adults after the kids are in bed.

Don't forget that novelty is also stimulating for children. Consider putting together a filing box of special projects for such times—this could contain recipes of things you and your child could cook together, instructions for a treasure hunt, or maybe a challenge to make three musical instruments out of household objects. Many books are available that are full of suitable suggestions.

The children's storybook series *My Naughty Little Sister* has a brilliant idea that you can easily copy. While convalescing, the little sister is given access to a special box of treasures assembled by a friendly neighbor. The box contains a series of intriguing but everyday items: a beautiful shell, a paper fan, a miniature doll. Each treasure is individually wrapped and packed in a compartment of a special chest. The reason why the box keeps the story's heroine so happily occupied is because it comes out only on rare occasions. Consequently, its contents retain an aura of special fascination.

Whether or not you make your own treasure chest, the principle of holding back a selection of toys or games that are brought out only on selective occasions is a good one. It can provide a really useful resource for when bored children need stimulation. Many of today's children are completely deluged with gifts at Christmas and birthdays. Why not increase your child's enjoyment and impact by staggering access to them through the year? If you introduce this principle early on, your kids will never know anything different. In retrospect, I wish I had adopted this policy with my two.

Have some toys or games that are not brought out frequently, and/or give your children new toys or games regularly throughout the year rather than all at once on their birthdays.

Facing Your Fear!

In the next section, we look at some simple techniques you can teach your child to help tackle the anxious thinking that can easily erode acceptable behavior.

With all fears and phobias, one of the keys to getting past them is helping children stop avoiding what they fear. You will remember from the cognitive model that thoughts, feelings, and behavior can all influence each other. Every time we avoid what we fear, we are giving our brains the message that we are "keeping ourselves safe." Because it stands to reason that we need to keep ourselves safe only from things that are hazardous, our self-protective behavior actually reinforces our sense of danger.

This is exactly what happened to eight-year-old Timothy. Ever since some friends in Halloween costumes had surprised him on the doorstep, he had become so terrified of masks that he couldn't walk past the costume shops in his local town without breaking out in a sweat. As a result, he kept himself away from anything associated with masks and monsters, and his phobia was becoming more limiting for him.

A very basic technique called graded exposure helped Timothy confront his fears. The first stage was to help him create his personal "ladder of fear." This consisted of a list of mask-related experiences and tasks that he thought would range from being mildly anxiety-provoking to absolutely terrifying for him. At the bottom end of Timothy's hierarchy were actions such as simply talking about masks, midway were actions such as looking at pictures of non-Halloween masks, and at the top of his list was the prospect of walking into one of the costume shops and handling a zombie mask.

Over the weeks, we worked through the stages from the bottom up. At each stage, Timothy found that after an initial peak in his anxiety levels, his fears subsided. His mind was slowly re-educating itself: Nothing bad was happening, and with help, he was able to keep himself in a more relaxed state. Gradually, the "frightening" experiences were being reclassified as safe. Moreover, Timothy was learning that his predictions about how frightening a particular stage would be were not always accurate. Within a few weeks, he was able to walk into the costume shop and handle a truly horrible-looking latex mask without great difficulty.

If you use this approach with your own child, make sure that you have enough stages in your hierarchy, that you have been specific about each different stage, and that the elements appear in the right order, from easiest to most difficult. When you work your way through, make sure your child has achieved a calm, controlled state at each level before moving on. Otherwise, the whole thing will backfire. It is also important that you are able to demonstrate each step yourself in a collected, relaxed fashion. If you have a phobia of spiders yourself, you may not be the right person to help your child with hers—unless, of course, you have already successfully completed a suitable desensitization program yourself.

If your child is frightened of something, help her face her fear by breaking it down into a series of manageable steps.

What If?

Anxiety paints a future full of frightening possibilities. Anxious thinking often ends up formulated in children's heads as a list of fearful questions: "What if my mommy doesn't get better?" "What if I fail my school tests?" "What if everyone laughs at my braces?" While these are valid questions, children gripped by fear seldom provide themselves with realistic answers. When children watch TV monsters through a crack in their fingers, they are obeying two seemingly contradictory laws of fear: Law 1: "Avoid the thing that frightens you"; and Law 2: "Keep what frightens you in sight at all times." These "what if?" thoughts also allow children to keep half an eye on their fears while preventing themselves from taking in the whole picture.

A terrifying prospect is like a movie film in which the frame usually freezes at the point when the anxiety becomes overwhelming. Children become fixated, finding it hard to move the film beyond the paralyzing image of the crowd of jeering faces, the dreaded results envelope, or the awful moment when they stand on that stage and cannot remember their next line. Their fear tells them that these events would be unbearable and that they would have no way of coping. This is rarely the case. One of the ways in which you can help a child deal with such fears is to encourage him to look squarely at the worst-case scenario and replace the question "What if?" with the question "What then?."

Alisha is a shy nine-year-old with a vivid imagination. Over recent weeks, she has become uncharacteristically sullen and moody. Last Tuesday, she was found in the shopping mall with a couple of her friends when she should have been at school. For her mother, this is the last straw and she has brought Alisha for counseling.

When I ask Alisha if anything has been bothering her recently, she eventually tells me that she has overheard her parents fighting almost every evening for the last week. Notice how the conversation is steered to help Alisha confront her fears while also exploring what resources she has available to cope with her worst-case scenario:

Me: So your Mom and Dad are arguing quite a lot?

Alisha: Yes.

Me: Well, there could be a lot of reasons for that. But what do you think it means?

Alisha: Well, they obviously can't stand the sight of each other if they can't be in the same room without shouting at each other all the time.

Me: Okay, well, that's certainly one possibility. But if you're right, **what is the worst thing about that?**

Alisha: It's how it always starts, isn't it?

Me: How what starts?

Alisha: You know …. [*She stares down at the floor and looks angry.*] How long will this take?

Me: Look, I appreciate that this is really hard to think about, Alisha, but if you can just stick with it, I want to see if we can help you feel a bit less frightened.

Instead of trying to push it out of your mind, **let's think together about the *very* worst thing that could happen.** What are you picturing in your head?

Alisha: That they split up, of course.

Me: Alright. Let's pretend you're right. **What would happen then?**

Alisha: Well, my life would be ruined. It would be horrible.

Me: I imagine that you might feel very unhappy. **But what would happen then?**

Alisha: I would be sad forever.

Me: Forever? Even when you're a grown-up?

Alisha: Yes, even then. Well, for a *really* long time, anyway.

Me: Hmmm. **So what would be the worst part of it, do you think?**

Alisha: My dad moving out.

Me: **What would be so bad about that?**

Alisha: Mala and I wouldn't see him every day.

Me: Probably not. **How would you cope with not seeing him every day?**

Alisha: I wouldn't have a choice. I'd just have to get used to it, I suppose ... but I'm not sure I ever would.

Me: It might be really hard to get used to. But if that *did* happen—your dad moves out—**is there anything you could do to make it a bit better for you and Mala?**

Alisha: Just have to make the most of the times we did see him, I suppose. Maybe he would get a place of his own like David's dad, and we could stay over sometimes. We could still talk to him on the phone every night, I guess. We could make him cards .... But you don't understand—it's not what I want. It just wouldn't be the same.

153

Me: You're absolutely right. It wouldn't be the same. It's the last thing you want to happen, and maybe it won't. But the point is, if it did, after a while **you would find ways to deal with it.**

Alisha: I was really sad when Grandma died, and I thought that would never stop.

Me: **What helped you then?**

Alisha: Just talking to my mom about it.

Me: Do you think you would talk to your mom about how you would feel if your dad left? What about other people? Do you know anyone else whose dad doesn't live at home anymore?

Alisha: Oh yes, loads of people in my class. Natalie's dad moved out last year, and she seems okay now. But it's different when it's your own family.

Me: Yes, it is. But the point is that your life would go on. And you would find ways to make it okay in the end because you are that kind of person, too. Does it still seem so terrifying when you think about it now?

Alisha: Not as frightening, exactly. Just really, really sad.

Teaching your children to look squarely at the very worst that could happen is, paradoxically, one of the techniques they often find the most calming. Encouraging children to think beyond the point of crisis and consider what they could do to help themselves make the best of a bad situation reminds them that they're not completely powerless and reduces anxiety levels.

Talk a child through something that worries them, using "what if?" and "what then?" to explore the worst-case scenario.

How Likely Is It?

Fear is very persuasive. It can make even the most unlikely scenarios seem like certainties. When frightened, most children do not even consider the other ways in which a given situation could work out because they remain fixated on the fearful outcome. In reality, every event—good or bad—depends on a whole sequence of other events taking place first.

If I work as a doctor in a hospital, you can safely assume that I have been to medical school, that I have passed my medical board exams, and that I have been successful in applying for a job there. These are all *necessary conditions* of my working there. Each anxiety scenario in your child's head also has a number of necessary conditions that must be met, although we seldom stop to analyze them when we are stressed or panicky. Nor do we pause to think about the routes that would fulfill these criteria or, more important, how likely each of these pathways is. In a child's head, feared possibilities can easily become certainties. Teaching your child to dismantle and rate the likelihood of these scenarios can be a really helpful way to ground him.

Eleven-year-old Cassie had developed an obsessive anxiety that her father would be killed in a car crash on his way back from work. Every time she closed her eyes, she pictured him bleeding to death in a heap of mangled wreckage at the side of the road. As a result, she couldn't sleep until he returned to the house, which was often late at night.

Her mother helped Cassie to think systematically about the pieces that needed to be in place in order to bring about the dreaded event. She realized that there were two necessary conditions without which the feared scenario was impossible: a) her father had to be involved in a crash in the first place, and b) he had to be so badly injured that the crash proved fatal.

Working together, Cassie and her mother came up with as many different pathways to fulfill the two necessary conditions as they could think of. Their list of factors potentially contributing to her father's involvement in an accident included these:

- ➤ Driving too fast

- ➤ Falling asleep at the wheel

- ➤ Being unable to avoid another out-of-control driver

- ➤ Blowing a tire or skidding on wet pavement

- ➤ Talking on the cell phone and losing concentration

By carefully exploring each of these possibilities in turn, Cassie was able to think more realistically about the likelihood of each one. She started monitoring how fast her father drove when she was in the car with him. Did he ever break the speed limit? What were her dad's views about people who did? Did she ever see him not wearing his seatbelt? By playing a game involving hand slaps with her father, Cassie established to her satisfaction that his reaction times were pretty quick, thereby reducing in her mind the likelihood that he would fail to respond swiftly if another car veered across the road.

Researching accurate factual information also helped Cassie rate the probability of the second necessary condition (her father being killed in the accident) more objectively. Using Department of Transportation data, she discovered that, even if involved in a road accident, as a driver, her father had a less than one in a hundred chance of being fatally injured.

By systematically breaking the feared scenario into its necessary conditions and then separately rating as a percentage the realistic probability of each contributing factor, Cassie found that the chances of *any* of the pathways she could imagine were much less than her fears were telling her. Moreover, because two necessary conditions were at play, if each was independently quite unlikely, then the necessary combination of the two was even more improbable. In other words:

Unlikely event A × Unlikely event B = *Very unlikely* event C

As you will gather, the more necessary conditions that have to be met to bring about a particular disaster, the less chance it will happen (unless all the necessary conditions are highly likely to be met).

Even for much younger children, learning to look at the various components involved in the scenario they fear can be useful. If there are aspects of their anxieties that can be tested, then by all means set up your own mini-experiments. If there is factual information that your child can use to combat her fears, then make sure she has access to it. All these activities strengthen "cool processing" capacities and can help your child rein in an overactive imagination.

Self-Soothing Techniques

Simple self-soothing techniques are one of the most useful tools you can give your child. Most are easy and unobtrusive enough for your child to use in any settings, and they really do work. In the case of babies and toddlers, we instinctively provide our children with what they need to decrease levels of agitation and distress. We hold them close to us, talk soothingly to them, and use a rhythmic rocking or patting motion to restore their equilibrium. We might provide them with a distraction and give them something else to focus on. We do all these things instinctively and automatically. However, as our children grow older, they are increasingly left to their own devices when it comes to dealing with escalating levels of internal stress.

Taking a Breather

Teaching your child to control his breathing takes only a few minutes, but studies show that deliberately practicing the right kind of breathing is one of the easiest ways to reduce tension and induce a relaxed, calm state.

Different kinds of breathing are associated with different emotional states. When we are tense, frightened, or anxious, we tend to breathe in rapid, shallow breaths, using our chest muscles to expand and contract our lungs. When we are relaxed, our breathing is naturally smooth, deep, and rhythmical. Relaxed breathing is coordinated by the muscles of the diaphragm—the wall between the chest and stomach cavity—and it draws air deep into the lungs.

The fact is that it is very hard for the body to remain in a state of tension while diaphragmatic breathing is taking place. Diaphragmatic breathing is a powerful cue for the parasympathetic nervous system, the system designed to restore calm and tranquility after the sympathetic nervous system has worked up to a state of high arousal. Diaphragmatic breathing sends a message to your body to stand down from red alert. The mind-body connection means that as you calm yourself physically, the mind automatically settles, too.

Whether your child is feeling stressed, panicky, or angry, if she knows how to breathe properly, or she will be taking an important step toward restoring her equilibrium and short-circuiting the arousal that goes with emotional hot processing.

Deep-breathing techniques can give your child an instant calming technique for times of distress.

To demonstrate this technique, get your child to place a hand on his stomach, just below his ribcage. Instruct him to focus on his hand and take a slow, deep breath through his nose. Ask him to picture drawing air into his lungs so that they fill from the bottom. If he is doing this properly, he should be able to feel his stomach pushing out slightly as the diaphragm depresses, and there should be only a minimal rise and fall of his chest cavity.

Now encourage your child to breathe in slowly to a count of five, hold the breath for a few seconds, and then slowly exhale to another count of five. For children who struggle with this, it can be helpful to get them to focus on the out breath rather than the inhalation. Ask your child to imagine that he has a lit candle a foot in front of him and that his job is to make the flame flicker just slightly for as long as he can, without blowing it out until his lungs are empty. Remind him that when he needs to refill his lungs, he should do so slowly through his nose. The sustained exhalation requires using the diaphragm in a way that usually kicks off diaphragmatic breathing.

When your child has mastered the art of diaphragmatic breathing, also let him know that, for it to have a reliable impact on his feelings, he will need to do at least three sets of ten breaths. Counting down from ten to one while he does so also has a helpful calming effect on most people. Next time you feel yourself getting worked up, try diaphragmatic breathing for yourself. You will be impressed by the difference it makes.

Using Progressive Muscle Relaxation

This simple technique is based on the work of Edmund Jacobson, a doctor who discovered that, by successively tensing and releasing different muscle groups throughout the body, it was possible to induce a state of deep relaxation that really helped patients with conditions such as high blood pressure, insomnia, and colitis. Interestingly, later studies have established that *regular* practice of deep relaxation using this technique can increase people's sense of control over their emotions, as well as boost self-esteem and improve all manner of anxiety symptoms.

Find a quiet place and a regular time for you and your child to practice this technique together. Before bed is an ideal time, especially because it's preferable not to use this technique on a full stomach. With younger children, it can be good to do a shortened form of this when they're in bed, so they can hopefully drift off into a relaxed sleep.

1. First, get your child to do a quick body scan and see whether she can detect any areas of particular tension. Tell her that she doesn't have to change anything, just notice what she finds.

2. Start by encouraging your child to clench her fists as tight as possible and hold it for 5 to 7 seconds. When she does let go, encourage her to let her hands go completely limp. Throughout the state of tension and the state of release, ask your child to concentrate on what she can feel in the relevant part of her body.

3. Move on to the biceps by getting your child to flex her forearms toward her shoulders, as if lifting a heavy weight. Again get her to hold the position for a few seconds and then release. In between muscle groups, spend about 20 seconds just focusing her awareness on the steady rise and fall of her breathing.

4. The triceps can be tensed by extending the arms outward and locking the elbows.

5. The forehead can be tensed by raising the eyebrows as high as possible.

6. Next, get your child to screw her eyes shut as tight as she can and then relax.

7. Opening the jaw as wide as possible (the "shark mouth"!) stretches the relevant muscles.

8. Get your child to pull her head back into the floor or pillow as much as she can to tense and release the muscles around the neck. When she releases this, encourage her to think of her head as something

really heavy, like a cannon ball just resting there, trying to sink into the floor.

9. Hunch the shoulders up to the ears and release.

10. Ask your child next to see whether she can make her shoulder blades touch, and then let go.

11. Use a deep breath to expand the chest and hold it tense for a count of five. Then release.

12. Then suck the stomach in as far as it will go. Let the tension flow away.

13. Arch the lower back.

14. Squeeze the buttocks together as tightly as possible—always guaranteed to produce a laugh.

15. Clench the thighs.

16. Flex the feet to produce a stretch in the calf muscles. Again let it go.

17. Ask your child to curl up her toes as much as she can.

18. Finally, get her to repeat the body scan and check that nothing is still tight or tense. Instruct her to follow the gentle rise and fall of her breathing and enjoy the sensations of comfort and relaxation.

To enjoy the maximum benefits, ideally, this routine should be practiced for about 20 minutes a day. Now, I am well aware this is not a realistic proposition for many busy parents. However, even if you use an abbreviated version of this technique, perhaps just concentrating on one or two muscle groups, you are still laying the foundation of a useful skill. You might also consider making your child a personalized relaxation tape so that she can practice on her own.

Learning to tense and release different muscles is relaxing for both body and mind.

If your child is in a situation in which he needs to calm down, just getting him to clench the hands and forearms as tight as he can for a few seconds before letting go provides a simple physical ritual for discharging excess stress. As with diaphragmatic breathing, even a partial experience of muscle relaxation can coax body and mind into a more composed state.

Just Imagine...the Calming Power of Visualization

The last two methods of self-soothing involved changing a physical state to affect a mental one. With visualization, the direction is reversed: The resources of the mind are used to dampen the body's stress reaction. The mind is very powerful, and the power of suggestion alone has enabled people to sit through painful dental treatment without analgesia. The robustness of the placebo effect—the fact that simply believing you are taking a helpful drug works in many cases as well as taking an actual drug—testifies to how a state of mind can influence our experience and even alter our physical state.

If your child becomes sufficiently practiced at using creative visualization techniques, she will be able to use this technique to calm herself. However, as with all these techniques, I would emphasize that the more your child practices, the more effective she will be when she needs to rely on them.

Visualization alone is sufficiently powerful to put most people into a relaxed state. If most people spend five minutes picturing themselves lying on a beautiful, sunlit beach, their heart rate drops, their respiration rate changes, and the level of electrical resistance that can be measured by skin sensors increases. Their brains also start generating more alpha waves, a pattern of activity associated with meditation, daydreaming, and deep relaxation.

Retreating to a Safe Place

"Whenever things get difficult at school or Jody is mean to me, I just go to my grandma's house and I always feel better," said Alice, looking earnestly at me through her deep green eyes. "That's great," I said, thinking to myself how helpful it was that Alice evidently had such a close, supportive relationship with her grandmother. However, when I later reported this back to her mother, she looked a bit perplexed. "Alice did have a really close bond with my mother," she told me, "but she died four years ago." Only then did I realize that Alice had spontaneously come up with a solution often taught to children who are having difficulty managing their feelings: She had created a mental refuge into which she could retreat whenever toxic emotions such as anxiety or fear threatened to take control.

Why not help your child create an imaginary sanctuary of his own? He may want to base this on a particularly pleasant memory, a time in his life when he felt especially secure and happy. Try to avoid memories of anywhere too active or stimulating. However good a time you all had on Space Mountain at Disneyland, it probably isn't the ideal focus for this kind of meditation. If your child is having difficulty thinking of a real time and place, feel free to encourage him to create one. It just has to be somewhere that feels safe and relaxing. Children I have known have chosen locations ranging from caves to jungles, although a tropical beach is always a good default option.

Encourage your child to visualize herself in a relaxing setting—and, ideally, create a personal "safe place" she can think about when the need arises.

The two keys to making the safe place visualization work for your child are

1. Linking it to a state of physical relaxation, perhaps using the breathing exercises or progressive muscle relaxation techniques just reviewed.

2. Making the scene as vivid as possible. Ideally, your child needs to flesh out the detail using all five senses. What colors and textures can he see? What does the sand feel like underfoot? What is the temperature like? Is there a breeze blowing over his skin, or is everything perfectly still? Can he smell the pine needles in the forest?

As he develops the scene, deliberately draw your child's attention to how he feels within it. Use words such as *relaxed, calm,* and *peaceful* in the description. Get your child to notice how his body feels when he thinks about this scene—how comfortable it feels to be there and how heavy and slack his limbs have become. Get him to tune into the steady rhythm of his heartbeat and the gentle rise and fall of his breathing.

After a few minutes, ask him to come up with a single word that summarizes the scene and what he is feeling. Ask him to touch the thumb and forefinger of his right hand together while he repeats that word silently in his mind.

If your child practices this for five minutes a day, before long, the simple act of bringing together his thumb and forefinger and saying his anchor word will be sufficient to conjure up the sense of relaxation associated with the safe place. He can then use this to counteract waves of panic, anger, acute stress, or general anxiety when they occur. The really good news is that studies suggest the generalization effects of a regular relaxation practice mean that he is also less likely to experience these emotions in such an intense form.

For many children, the knowledge that there is something they can do to bring themselves back into a more collected state is a great comfort. When they have overcome the initial hurdle of practicing sufficiently for the image to produce a reliable effect, even very young children say that it makes a real difference, and many like to think about their safe place just before they go to sleep.

More Visualization Ideas to Combat Anxiety

In Chapter 3, "Mind Control for Beginners," we looked at how beneficial it can be for a child to personify the source of negative emotions in his life and invent a magical solution to disarm it. You can also enlist visualization techniques to replace one emotion with another. The following are just a few suggestions for images that children can use. Feel free to invent your own together.

The Hourglass

Get your child to picture her anxious feelings as bright red sand in an old-fashioned egg timer (you might have to get hold of one if your child doesn't know what this is). Explain that, however hard they might try, the grains of sand cannot stay in the upper chamber. Encourage your child to imagine her anxiety passing slowly through the neck of the hourglass under gravity's influence until the top chamber is completely empty. Repeat this process until your child feels calmer. A similar image to explore is bathwater swirling down the plug. Don't rush this one: Picturing the slow trickle of the sand or water over a sustained period gives the parasympathetic nervous system time to do its work.

Lighten Up

For this visualization, ask your child to imagine unwanted stressful feelings as a sickly, pulsing color radiating outward from wherever he feels the anxiety most strongly in his body. This will usually be the solar plexus or the head. Make sure your child has a clear mental image of this before you move on to the next stage.

As your child breathes in using the diaphragmatic breathing described earlier, ask him to imagine that he is drawing cool, pure light into his body from a point at the top of his head. As he breathes, help him picture the cleansing light becoming steadily stronger and brighter, working its way through the cells of his whole body.

As his body fills with light, ask him what is happening to the anxious colored mist he began with. Some children naturally picture the light neutralizing the mist as it grows more intense. Others talk about the white light "pushing the mist out." Work with whatever your child suggests, but emphasize that the two cannot occupy the same space and that the white light is much more powerful. Keep going until your child can imagine his whole body pulsating with the white light and all traces of the anxiety mist dispelled. As with the hourglass, you may need to repeat this exercise several times before the desired result is achieved.

> Use guided visualization techniques to help your child get rid of anxious feelings by imagining them draining away—or being pushed out by something stronger and more positive.
>
>

Mental Dress Rehearsals

If your child is anxious about a specific future event, it can be helpful to use visualization in much the same way sports psychologists encourage athletes to do before they run a race. Mentally rehearsing each step of the event in detail and picturing a positive outcome can shift children into a more optimistic mindset. This will also help them activate the inner resources that make the desired outcome more likely. If children are struggling to do this, the point at which their mental projection becomes derailed can often help identify the crux of the problem. Knowing this, you and your child can use problem-solving strategies discussed in Chapter 7 to come up with solutions to any specific difficulties.

Lifestyle Issues

Physically active children tend to be less stressed than passive ones. Exercise can play a valuable role in building children's resistance to stress, and all the research figures are suggesting that our children play fewer sports and spend more time in front of various screens than ever before. Only one in ten children currently achieves the 90 minutes a day currently recommended by the government. Find out what physical activities your child enjoys and create opportunities for her to pursue them. Do physically demanding things together and make such activities part of your family life.

Yoga is a particularly good way of teaching children to relax, and it has several other health benefits. There are many good children's yoga classes dotted around the country, and they can be particularly helpful for children who find it hard to be still and quiet. So just because you cannot imagine your child fitting into such a class, don't rule it out. The fact that they are surrounded by other engaged children, combined with the fact that they will have to concentrate to hold some of the positions successfully, can have a transformative effect. Again, if you have an established yoga or meditation practice of your own, your child is likely to be much more receptive to the idea of joining in.

The role that diet might play in relation to childhood stress has yet to be conclusively resolved. However, nutrition experts such as Alexander Schauss believe that a diet that is excessively rich in unrefined carbohydrates requires more B vitamins than the body often has available, with the result that such vitamins are "borrowed" from the nervous system. Schauss argues that this can increase susceptibility to stress and lead to all manner of behavioral problems. There is also some evidence that removing junk food from the diets of children with Attention Deficit Hyperactivity Disorder (ADHD) can help some children, although results from these studies are not consistent.

What is clear is that if children eat a lot of sugary foods, they can end up trapped into a boom-bust cycle of sugar rushes. These are hard for the body to cope with and can also lead to manic, out-of-control behavior. Although we have yet to fully understand the relationship between diet and the nervous system, suffice it to say that a healthy, balanced diet is more likely to provide the brain with the nutrients it needs to function well.

Finally, make sure your child is getting enough sleep. It is no coincidence that sleep deprivation is one of the methods used to stress torture victims. A school-age child needs an average of ten hours sleep, and preschoolers need more than this. Be aware that, due to a perversity of the adolescent body clock, teenagers are naturally inclined to go to bed later and wake later in the morning, a fact not accommodated by the schedule of the school day. This means that your adolescent child might have to train himself to rest at times when his body clock is telling him otherwise. Good sleeping habits are a discipline that has to be learned. Many parents these days let children dictate their own bedtimes, and this is a big mistake. Children often think they need less sleep than they do, and a tired child is much more vulnerable to stress and much more likely to be cranky and short-tempered.

Don't Leave It to Chance

To sustain "good behavior," a child must subdue all kinds of urges and instincts. This is hard work that makes real demands on his mental resources. Stress has been defined as the state that occurs "when a situation exceeds our available resources to cope." If your child is already stressed, she will find it extremely difficult to deal with any additional demands made of her. In practice, this means that a stressed or anxious child is inevitably much more likely to be a badly behaved one.

In view of this, keeping an eye on your child's stress levels and giving him practical strategies to manage stress is essential if you don't want to end up in the company of a child who can no longer regulate his own conduct—a sure-fire recipe for raising your own stress levels!

You cannot shield your child from the stresses of life, but you can give her skills to disarm and diffuse their effects. You wouldn't send a soldier into battle without adequate protection, but that is precisely what we often do to children when we send them into the world without knowing how to handle stress and anxiety properly. Some people work out ways to help themselves, but the process of trial and error can be a long and costly business. It is far better to equip your children with stress-management tools while they still have their lives ahead of them than wait for a nervous breakdown, relationship failure, or heart attack to provide an unwelcome wake-up call in adulthood. Being stressed and anxious is a miserable experience. As a parent, you have an opportunity to make a real difference in your child's quality of life (and your own) by taking the time to teach these basic skills. It is well worth it.

Quick Summary Action Points

- Learn to recognize the signs of a child under stress.

- Be careful what you let your child watch on TV—children can worry about things more than you might think.

- Be conscious of potential pressures at school. Don't place an unhealthy emphasis on achievement.

- Tread carefully around your child's "symbols of self" and be sensitive to underlying insecurities.

- Recognize that children often find change stressful and prepare your child if a change is on the horizon.

- Too much stimulation can be stressful—and so can too little. Help your child understand what she needs and help her to achieve the right balance.

- Consider using graded exposure to help your child face his fears.

- Diffuse anxiety by getting your child to look squarely at the worst-case scenario instead of avoiding it.

- Help your child calculate the likelihood of the things she fears.

- Help your child master self-soothing techniques such as diaphragmatic breathing, progressive muscle relaxation, and visualization.

- Make sure your child's lifestyle is designed to keep stress levels low.

Six

People Powers:
Cultivating Social Confidence

Whether or not you agree with Sartre that "hell is other peo-ple," if children are unable to relate well to others, this can make life very difficult for them and those around them. Human beings are supremely social animals, and we live our whole lives entangled with the lives of others. "Bad behavior" often occurs when children's ability to relate appropriately breaks down. This means that equipping kids with tools to negotiate the complex world of human relationships has to be a priority for any parent who wants his child to cope with the strong emotions other people can trigger. Being able to engage successfully with others and control your reactions to them is a prerequisite of a fulfilled, happy life.

In this chapter, we look at how you can help your children stay in control when provoked, and how you can coach them in the principles of clear and assertive communication so they can handle other children more confidently. We also take a brief look at the dynamics of groups and think about how you can help your children to feel they belong without getting caught up in the more destructive undercurrents of group life.

We start by focusing on managing an emotion that can wreak havoc with your child's relationships and behavior both inside and outside the family. Children are particularly vulnerable to it, but, if left unchecked, this emotion can also establish habits that will do real damage to their adult lives as well. This emotion is anger.

The Upside of Anger

Because of its destructive power, anger has received very bad press. It is true that the anger of children is responsible for some of the most mortifying moments of parenthood: An enraged child is capable of saying and doing just about anything. Nevertheless, your children need to understand that anger is a perfectly normal emotion that we all experience and that only *uncontrolled* anger leads to such undesirable consequences. To better understand the more positive face of anger, let's briefly consider the circumstances under which children tend to see red.

Children usually get angry in three situations. First, when they feel under attack—either physically or verbally—anger galvanizes them to strike back. Just as the puffer fish instantly inflates itself to several times its resting size when threatened, angry behavior warns potential predators to back off. The difficulty is that the limbic system of the brain, which drives the anger response, does not pause to calibrate the true extent of the threat, so the reaction can be completely out of proportion to the original cause.

Second, children often become angry and frustrated when they are blocked from achieving their goals. This is why it so often difficult for children to play together. Successful collaboration inevitably involves a trade-off between your own needs and those of the people you are playing with. Keeping control under such circumstances is very difficult for some children, as a million overturned board games can testify. This is also why practicing self-control within the context of play is so valuable.

Third, children are easily angered by situations in which they feel their rights are being violated. The universal childhood protest of "It's not fair!" often heralds an angry outburst. Children are wedded to principles such as fairness, honesty, and responsibility (in other people, at least) not least because they depend on such values to police the way other people treat them. In situations where these principles are not enforced, children know they are vulnerable.

In each case, anger is serving a valid self-protective function. Anger is designed to protect us against the encroachments of other people, to maintain our sense of personal power and hold others accountable if they overstep the mark. In themselves, these are all worthy aims, but your child needs to understand that to keep his anger from backfiring and causing more problems than it solves, it needs to be appropriate to the circumstance and, more importantly, harnessed in a controlled fashion.

Race Against the Clock

Children who struggle with anger need to know that they have only a few seconds in which to act if they are to stand any chance of retaining self-control. For many, there swiftly comes a point of no return beyond which all chance of self-restraint is lost.

For this reason, it is essential that your child become very familiar with the tell-tale signs of an impending explosion. These symptoms vary among individuals, so when the dust settles after your child's next eruption, sit down and help her identify the changes that let her know she is about to flare up. The warning signs can be physical, emotional, or cognitive. The following is a list of some of the symptoms children report, but be aware that your own child might be conscious of others or conceive them in her own unique style:

➤ "My heart beats really fast."

➤ Feeling of tightness in the chest

➤ "I can't catch my breath."

➤ Butterflies in the stomach

➤ Muscle tension

➤ "It's like this ball in my tummy gets heavier and heavier."

➤ Sensation of pressure around the head

➤ Feeling wound up inside

➤ Increased agitation: "I start to get really fidgety."

➤ "The other person's face gets really big, like in a close-up."

➤ Fists clenching

➤ Sensation of "building pressure"

➤ Feeling slightly sick

➤ Prickly heat on the back of the neck

➤ "I hear bad words ... swears in my head."

➤ Problems thinking straight

➤ Sensation of things closing down—tunnel vision

➤ Red mist descending

➤ "I get this roaring sound in my ears."

➤ "I picture myself hurting the other person really bad."

➤ "Remembering other times when I got really angry"

➤ Wave of sudden, unnatural stillness: the calm before the storm

➤ "My feelings switch off just before it takes over."

Explain to your child that the nature of anger means he cannot afford to hang around. The minute he starts to notice any of his personal warning signs, he needs to act decisively and quickly using the traffic light rule.

The Traffic Light Rule

The presence of any of these anger symptoms is an automatic red light. The moment your child detects them, she needs to *STOP* what she is doing *immediately* and remove herself from the situation so she can regain control. Anger is often linked to a particular setting, and physically removing yourself from that place is one of the most effective steps you can take to reduce its intensity.

If your child is in a situation in which it is impossible to leave, she can achieve some sense of distance by imagining herself viewing the scene (still with her in it) as if she is looking down from a corner of the ceiling. Shifting perspective like this and viewing the situation from the outside creates detachment and engages "cool" processing mechanisms that automatically make the nervous system less reactive. Reassure your child that getting out is not the same as opting out. She can still address the problem that led to the mounting anger when she has regained control. In fact, it is important that she does so. More about this shortly.

Train your children to spot their anger warning signs—and to stop whatever they are doing immediately when the signs appear, ideally by leaving the room or situation.

The yellow light phase is the one your child uses to restore his equilibrium. Diaphragmatic breathing and safe place visualization is invaluable during this stage (see Chapter 5, "Wrestling with Monsters: Overcoming Stress and Anxiety,"), but the key is to delay response, perhaps using a tactic as simple as counting down slowly from 20.

An image that children of all ages find useful is to think of their anger as a leaking bucket with holes in the bottom. Stressful situations can pour in water so fast that, unless we are careful, the bucket will overflow. However, if we can stop adding to the bucket and just wait, even if we do nothing else, the water that is already there will trickle out. Anger tells our brains that we need to follow through right away. If we exercise self-control and do nothing, our lack of response eventually means that our emotions fall into line with what are body is doing (or, in this case, *not* doing).

For children who have trouble calming themselves, one trick they can try is sucking a piece of hard candy. This works because the sucking reflex is associated with states of calm and comfort in newborn children. Also, the brain cannot experience states of pleasure and fury at the same time, so if your child is enjoying the flavor of something in his mouth, it will be more difficult for her to remain quite as worked up.

> Use tactics to help release anger, such as sucking a piece of hard candy, counting slowly, or simply waiting and doing nothing until the anger subsides.
>
>

The yellow light phase also gives your child the chance to review the situation and ask herself the following crucial questions:

➤ Why am I angry?

➤ How angry do I feel? (Score this from 1 to 10.)

➤ How angry (out of 10) *should* I feel in this situation?

➤ What will happen to *me* if I give in to my anger right now?

➤ Can I think of a way of getting what I need that doesn't involve me losing control?

179

Only when anger levels have dropped to a maximum of 2 or 3 out of 10 should your child give herself a green light to return to the original situation. When your child is back in control, this is the stage at which she needs to use assertive communication. At the very least, she needs to tell the person concerned how she felt and, if possible, negotiate a solution to the original conflict. Children who manage to diffuse their anger in the short term but don't find constructive ways to address the forces driving it often end up turning their rage inward and can become stressed and depressed.

> Help your child address the cause of the anger when he is calm, even if it's only telling the person who triggered it that he felt angry and why.
>
> **" "**

Are They Really Out to Get You?

If anger is a protective response, it stands to reason that angry people feel threatened a lot of the time. The way they think is one way in which angry children keep this sense of threat turned to maximum. If your child is prone to anger, he might need to train himself out of habits of thought that turn even the most innocent of situations into something more ominous.

"He was *deliberately* trying to wind me up by singing that song over and over again, so I had to hit him to make him stop." Hardly audible over the howls of his younger brother, this explanation was offered to me by my eldest son, who clearly believed that, under such circumstances, punching his brother was an entirely reasonable response.

My son was displaying of the most common thought habits of angry people: He had ascribed a malevolent motive almost guaranteed to trigger an aggressive response. Now, his brother loves to sing and does have a tendency to latch on to a particular phrase and repeat it *ad nauseam*, sometimes to the accompaniment of an exotic dance move of his own devising. After a while (and I hope he will forgive me for saying so in a public forum), this can be pretty irritating. However, my eldest leaped almost instantly from irritation to full-scale physical aggression because he convinced himself that my youngest had *intentionally* set out to annoy him. In his mind, that was the only possible meaning of his younger brother's action.

Admittedly, this might actually have been the case. However, the point is, my eldest was not in a mood to consider alternative explanations. Consequently, he neither pointed out the effect the song was having on him nor asked his brother to go sing it elsewhere. Assuming that it was intended to be a personal affront, he let his fists do the talking and got sent to bed early as a result.

This kind of mind-reading act is typical of the way angry people of all ages read other people's intentions. It is really important to encourage children to question their assumptions about other people's motives if you don't want them to be ruled by anger. Teach them to look for innocent explanation and extenuating circumstances.

Emotive Language

In a similar vein, help your child listen for the way she describes situations to herself. Angry people tend to see things in terms of extremes, and their language often reflects this. "It just shows that Charlie and Hakeem *hate* me, and I can't stand them. They're *so* selfish. They're my very worst enemies," complained Fergus, age six, about two of his classmates. When his father probed a bit further, it turned out that almost everything Fergus had just told him was blatantly untrue.

There was no evidence that Charlie and Hakeem "hated" Fergus, and the many hours the three boys had happily played together suggested it wasn't the case that Fergus couldn't "stand" them, either. Charlie and Hakeem had not even been especially "selfish"—they had just declined to swap a star-player football card for the lower-value cards Fergus was offering. However, when Fergus translated the situation into such powerfully emotive terms, he was halfway to convincing himself that these boys were his sworn enemies. Always watch out for language in your child's speech that accentuates a sense of threat, animosity, or rivalry, and teach him to be on guard against it.

> Help your child to see that irritating or hurtful events were not necessarily *designed* to irritate or hurt.
>
>

Maintaining the angry person's position that the world is a dangerous place full of people who want to harm or take advantage of you requires the opposite of rose-tinted glasses. Angry children focus on the evidence that supports their beliefs and ignore facts that don't fit. Help your child to use the sort of courtroom skills described in Chapter 3, "Mind Control for Beginners," to achieve a more objective evaluation of the situation.

What Is Assertive Communication?

Beth was one of the shyest ten-year-olds I have met. When she came into the room, she stared at the ground and said nothing at all for the first 20 minutes. I tried without success to ask her a few gentle questions. When I got no response, I started to speculate about what she might be feeling. I asked her to nod if I was on the right track. I continued in a similar vein until it occurred to me that Beth was simply agreeing with *everything* put to her. If I had suggested she had six heads and worked down a mine, she probably wouldn't have contradicted me. It came as no great surprise to learn that Beth was being bullied at school. One thing was clear: Whatever else was required, she needed to become much more assertive.

Assertiveness is a set of skills that help us stand up for ourselves without feeling overly anxious. They enable us to express ourselves clearly and defend our rights, while also behaving respectfully toward other people. Assertive communication involves a few basic principles that even young children can master, but many children are never taught them.

Ironically, the children who benefit most from assertiveness training are those usually considered to be the most forceful in their dealings with others. Angry, aggressive children often act this way because they lack confidence in their ability to get their needs met by any other means. They often fail to speak up before it is too late, stockpiling festering resentments that could have been diffused if the individual had been able to express his feelings clearly at the time.

It is crucial to teach your child the difference between being assertive and being aggressive. Many children find it hard to grasp the distinction. One of the most straightforward ways to do this is to think about the differences between the ways in which angry, confident, and shy people behave. Give your child the task of observing the people he meets, as well as thinking about characters in TV dramas, books, or comics. Ask him to think about the way people in these two categories use their bodies, as well as what they say and how they speak. Beth's list read as follows:

Aggressive/Angry	Confident	Shy
Shouty	Relaxed	Looks at floor
Swears at people	Looks you in the eye	Hunches over
Comes up too close	Speaks clearly	Doesn't speak much
Wags finger and points a lot	Stands tall	Apologizes even when things are not her fault
Fierce expression	Doesn't react	Hesitates
Threatening	Means what he says	Doesn't look at you
Blows up easily	Strong, not pushed around	Weak voice
Unpopular	Stays calm	Feels panicky
Rude	Shows feelings	Follows lead of other people
Looks out of control	Can say "no" and disagree	

Sounding Like You Mean It

When she had achieved a clearer idea about what she was aiming for, Beth had to work on the way she talked to people. She was asked to apply three simple principles:

1. Practice using "I" statements as much as possible.

2. Keep it concise.

3. Say it loud and clear.

Using "I" statements is usually a hallmark of assertive people. Nervous people lack the confidence to take ownership of their wishes and opinions, whereas aggression speaks a language of blame that focuses on the perceived failings of the other person: "*You* always put me down ...." "Why can't *you* be more understanding? "*You're* such a jerk!"

For children like Beth, learning to use phrases such as "*I* think" and "*I* feel" and "*I* want" can feel very exposing at first. Ironically, for such a bashful girl, Beth believed that if she used the first person like this, people would see her as selfish and egotistical. However, Beth soon found it empowering to communicate her views and feelings in a more direct, transparent way.

Beth also recognized that her tentative, rambling way of talking when she did speak was giving people the impression that they didn't have to take her seriously. She challenged herself to use as few words as possible when asking for things, even though she was worried this would sound rude. Rewarding her for dropping specific speech mannerisms, such as clearing her throat before she spoke and using hesitation phenomena (excessive use of "um" and "er"), also helped make her sound more focused and confident.

Beth also had a tendency to let her voice drift away at the end of sentences and allow the pitch to get higher, giving her speech a slightly whining, wheedling quality that made her sound weak. She corrected this by imagining the final word of her sentences as the bull's-eye toward which she was aiming a vocal arrow. She learned to target the end of the sentence with sufficient force, to prevent her delivery from drifting off course, and kept her tone more level. To keep her from being so soft-spoken, she was encouraged to visit a nearby motorway bridge and compete with the volume of the traffic.

Discuss the differences between aggressive, assertive, and shy behavior to your children and help them determine how to shift their behavior in the direction needed.

Looking Like You Mean It

It was not just Beth's verbal communication skills that were letting her down. Her stooped posture and avoidance of eye contact were also giving an unhelpful message. Instead of adopting the posture of the "hibernating hedgehog," Beth was encouraged to "face the gale." This involved standing as if a strong wind was blowing against her, planting her feet squarely on the deck, pulling her shoulders back, and holding her head up. Beth learned that although her averted gaze made her appear submissive, too much eye contact could be misinterpreted as threatening. She got used to holding the other person's gaze for a couple of seconds, glancing away momentarily, and then looking back. When she was making a strong "I" statement, Beth was reminded to make sure that she always ended her sentence looking directly at the other person.

A Winning Formula

Although by changing the way she presented herself Beth was starting to create a very different impression, the real test was whether she could use her new skills to deal with the constant teasing she faced at school. Previously when this occurred, Beth typically would say nothing and beat a hasty retreat. She needed to try something new. It was agreed that the next time one of the girls at school was unpleasant to her, she would use the following protocol:

1. Give a brief, factual description of the situation as she saw it.

2. Let the other person know how she felt in this situation using the formula "When you do X, I feel Y."

3. Make a strong statement of her own desire or need.

4. Give a clear warning about the action she would take if that need is not met.

When Beth arrived at her next session, I could tell she was pleased with herself. Apparently, the ring leader of the girls bullying her had made some snide remark about her appearance in the corridor as she passed by. Instead of pretending she had not heard, Beth confronted the girl and dealt assertively with the situation:

> I heard what you said about my clothes just now (step 1). When you make those kinds of comments, I feel upset and angry (step 2). I want you to stop making fun of me (step 3). If you don't stop, I am going straight to Miss Jenkins because I have had enough of all this (step 4)."

Impressively, she had not even waited for a reply, but turned smartly on her heels and walked briskly away. Beth could hear the other girls giggling in embarrassment behind her, but she reported that they had steered clear of her for the rest of that week. "To be honest," she said, "I don't really care if they keep going. I shouldn't care what people like that think about me anyway." Acting more assertively was affecting not only how Beth was perceived by others, but also how she was feeling about herself.

Know Your Rights

One of the reasons children often fail to stick up for themselves is simply because they're not clear about what they are entitled to expect from other people. It is worth helping school-age children compose a personal bill of rights so they can achieve some sense of clarity about this issue. Children need to decide what they are entitled to, what standards to maintain, and where the line falls between acceptable and unacceptable behavior.

We noted earlier that respect is a key component of assertiveness, but truly assertive behavior is not just about encouraging respectful behavior from others; it's also about demonstrating respect in your dealings with them. One of the benefits of taking the time to think about a personal bill of rights is that it also gives children clear guidelines as to how they can conduct themselves in ways that respect other people's rights, too.

When your child has come up with five to ten principles that he is happy with, take the time to type or write them out neatly.

Perhaps you can even frame the document and put it up some-where he will see it every day. Encourage your child to approach this task in his own way, but if the bill is to function as a useful benchmark for assertive behavior, it should proba-bly include some of the following principles:

I have a right...

> To say what I think

> To express my feelings and wishes

> To be treated with respect

> To live my life without being bullied or manipulated

> To be myself

> To stick up for my rights

> To respect the rights of others

> To use my talents and abilities

> To choose how I respond to other people

Keep in mind that the process of becoming more assertive and finding the delicate point between confidence and aggression is one that children can take a while to perfect. Sometimes the situations they encounter on the playground can challenge even the most assertive individual. Be on hand to provide extra support and coaching when needed.

Most children learn best by doing, so if you are attempting to help your child develop a more assertive demeanor, it is important to give him opportunities to practice the skills as much as possible. Prepare your child for encounters with aggressive or critical people by role-playing conflict situations beforehand. In the heat of the moment, it can be hard for children to remember what they should do, but if they are well rehearsed, the appropriate responses should come much more readily to mind.

> Use current real-life situations to "rehearse" the best things to say to handle situations assertively.
>
>

When your child does have to hold his ground, the following techniques can also be useful.

Playing the Broken Record

Let your child know that one of the keys to assertiveness is persistence. She needs to be able to deflect attempts to push her off course or derail her efforts to get her needs met. One of the simplest ways of doing this is to employ a technique referred to as the broken record. This simply involves calmly restating your position until the other person is forced to acknowledge it. It works most powerfully if the need can be expressed in a single, concise statement that can be repeated as many times as necessary—hence the term "broken record." Instead of engaging with the other person's arguments or distraction techniques, children using this technique simply restate their main point until their opponent gives up.

In this example, Danny uses the broken record technique to resist the pressure his friend Steven applies to let him copy his homework.

Steve: Come on, Danny.... Help me out here.... At least let me copy the last few questions. Mr. Wilson's going to kill me if I don't hand anything in this week. I'll owe you....

Danny: I'm really sorry, Steve. You're a good friend and I don't want you to get into trouble, but it doesn't feel right. *I just don't feel comfortable letting you copy my work.*

Steve: What's the harm in it? It's not going to cost you anything: You've done it already.

Danny: That's not the point. It took me ages. Besides, if you copy the answers, you're still not going to understand any of it.

Steve: So are you saying I'm stupid now?

Danny: No, I'm not. *I just don't feel comfortable letting you copy my work.*

Steve: You can be a real jerk sometimes. I've done loads of stuff for you. What about when I stood up for you against that eighth-grade kid? Or loaned you my Nintendo for all those weeks when you were sick?

Danny: I really appreciate those things, Steve, but this is different. *I just don't feel comfortable letting you copy.*

Steve: Maybe what you're really worried about is other people getting as good grades as you. Is that it? Poor little Danny worried he's not going to be top of the class? Not going to be King of the Class anymore?

Danny: Steve, you can try to wind me up all you want. *I don't feel comfortable about letting you copy.* It's not going to happen. Look, I can't help you this time, but if you want, we can study together next week.

Steve: I thought you were supposed to be my friend....

Danny: I am your friend, but—

Steve [mimicking Danny]: *"I don't feel comfortable about letting you copy my work."* I get it, alright? God, you're such a loser. [Steve storms off.]

Anyone using this technique, whether an adult or child, should be aware that it can prove highly frustrating for the other person. By refusing to be drawn in, Danny leaves Steve effectively beating his head against a brick wall. The broken record is a form of passive resistance and, although often effective, it can create considerable resentment. Normally, assertive communication always attempts to find a compromise that protects the self-esteem of both parties, but, as in this example, this is not always possible.

Explain that sometimes people will try to argue instead of accepting how you feel, and talk about how to hold your ground when this happens.

Fogging

In the martial art of Aikido, the student is taught that the most effective way to counter an attack is not to meet it head on, but to "blend" with the motion of the attacker. In doing so, you turn your opponent's strength against him. Fogging relies on a similar principle. The key is to search for something in your adversary's remarks that you can agree upon—at least, in principle. Most arguments involve disagreement and the defense of a fixed position by both parties. By fogging, your child aims to disarm her opponent by working to establish some common ground. Because this technique requires some sophistication and the ability to think quickly on your feet, it is usually more appropriate for older children.

In the following example, teenager Dinah uses a fogging technique to tackle a stream of put-downs from her brother Marcus.

Marcus: I can't believe you're on the computer again. Don't you ever do anything else but Facebook these days?

Dinah: You're right, my sweet little brother. I have been spending a lot of time at the computer recently. [*fogging*]

Marcus: Has it ever occurred to you that other people might want to use it sometimes?

Dinah: Perhaps I am being a bit selfish. [*fogging*]

Marcus: I'm surprised you and your loser friends have that much to say to each other.

Dinah: I can see that you might be surprised by that. [*fogging*]

Marcus: You're probably spending all your time talking about boyfriends. I don't know why: With a face like that, you're never going to get one!

Dinah: Mmmm. I can see that the way you feel about me might make it hard for you to imagine that anyone else might find me attractive. [*fogging*]

Marcus: You could at least make more of an effort with yourself.

Dinah: [smiles sweetly] You're absolutely right, Marcus. I probably could pay more attention to my appearance. [*fogging*]

Marcus: You're weirding me out, Sis. What's wrong with you today?

Dinah:	You have a point, Marcus. I certainly don't seem to be reacting to you like I usually do. [*fogging*] I appreciate that this might be making you feel uncomfortable. [*fogging*]
Marcus:	Mom! Dinah's freaking me out. Make her stop!

Fogging can be a very effective way of dealing with verbal bullying. When bullies use insults, they're trying to provoke a reaction. Although the content of a fogging response may look submissive because the attack isn't actively resisted, if the person using the technique can retain an aura of unperturbed calm, it can be very powerful.

In some cases, pushing agreement to a point at which it becomes ludicrous or comical can completely take the wind out of an aggressor's sails. One nine-year-old boy responded to a bully's taunt of "You're a girl, you're a girl" after missing a penalty soccer shot by responding, "Yes. You're absolutely right. I am completely female. Just look at my long flowing hair and girlish clothes. I am the biggest girl ever, and now I need to leave because I am late for a volleyball match. Do you want a kiss?" Everyone around fell down laughing, and the insult completely backfired.

Learning to Negotiate

On a daily basis, your child will encounter situations in which her own wishes and needs clash with those of other people. Learning how to handle these situations is a critical life skill that children need to start practicing as soon as possible. Try and reinforce the following principles whenever you have the opportunity:

➤ Help your child understand that life isn't a competition. It's not just about getting what you want, but about finding solutions in which everybody gets some of what they want. If two people have both given a bit of ground but leave happy, that's a much bigger success than getting your way but leaving another person feeling squashed.

➤ Emphasize that, for negotiations to work, it is essential to maintain a respectful and considerate attitude toward the other person. If people feel attacked, they will be in no mood to compromise.

➤ Remind your child that one way to do this is to openly and directly acknowledge the other person's feelings, needs, and concerns: "It's horrible to feel left out ... let's find a way to do it that's fair for everyone."

➤ Successful negotiation depends as much on listening as it does on talking. Encourage your child to ask questions that help him fully understand the other person's point of view.

➤ Stress the importance of keeping an open mind. Help your child to think flexibly and creatively in the search for solutions. Children can seem to be wearing blinders at times and assume that there is only one answer to a given problem. This is seldom the case.

➤ Reinforce the importance of keeping a cool head. If things are getting heated, teach your child that the best way forward could be to take a break for a few minutes and return to the negotiating table after everyone has calmed down.

You can lay the foundation of these skills with even very young children using games that teach the value of collaboration or compromise to achieve their goals. Comprehension and memory games in which competitors have to answer questions about narrated stories in return for candy or other token rewards can also train young infants to listen attentively. Simple piece-collecting games such as Go Fish or Beetle can be modified so that players can exchange missing pieces and have to bargain and compromise accordingly. Older children can learn much about negotiation principles from games such as Monopoly. The wheeling and dealing involved can nurture skilled negotiators, as well as provide useful lessons in how and why negotiations can so easily break down.

From an early age, your children can learn listening skills, negotiation, collaboration, and compromise from playing games.

Understanding Groups

Children's participation in groups molds their experience in profound ways. Chances are, the real highs and lows of your child's experience will be determined by what happens in groups, whether friendship groups, school classes, or the family. The importance of different groups waxes and wanes over the course of a child's development. We know, for example, that after the age of eight, friendship groups become enormously important and probably more influential than what happens at home. Because children cannot avoid groups, and because of the significant role they play in their lives, it makes sense for you and your child to understand something about the ways groups operate.

More Than Meets the Eye

Psychologists who have studied groups recognize that any group, regardless of size, is more than the sum of its parts. Groups have a powerful life of their own and can stir up primitive psychic energies with surprising ease. Psychotherapist Wilfred Bion devoted a large part of his professional life to studying groups—what he noticed was that groups seem to operate at two levels. On the surface, most groups have a job to do, and much group activity is naturally organized around this purpose or "group task." A school orchestra comes together to play and perform music, a class is created to organize its pupils so that they can learn, a football team comes together to play and win games, and so on.

However, Bion also observed that a lot of what goes on in groups is an expression of much more basic human drives and instincts. Despite surface differences, groups are preoccupied with very similar concerns: themes of dominance and control, rivalry and allegiance, belonging and exclusion.

Children need to be alert to the powerful forces groups can stir up in them and those around them. What is going on beneath the surface of the group can cause people to act in an extreme and irrational manner. Groups can generate enormous anxiety among their members and can cause people to act in uncharacteristic ways—which explains why your child might get along very well with another child when they are alone, but as part of a bigger group, their behavior might be completely different.

Julia and Samantha were best friends most of the time, but whenever they played together with other children, it was very obvious that Samantha missed no opportunity to put her friend down. She constantly made "jokes" about Julia's red hair and glasses, and even started parodying certain mannerisms. Quite understandably, Julia became really upset by this.

When Samantha was confronted about her behavior, at first she denied that anything was going on. She insisted that she was "just messing around." However, later that night, her mother found her crying in her room. When she asked her what was the matter, Samantha confessed that she knew that she was hurting her friend's feelings but added, "I just can't seem to stop myself, Mommy. The other girls think I'm funny, but the thing is, they're not even my friends—well, not like Julia is, anyway. I don't know what's wrong with me."

The answer is simply that Samantha had fallen under the spell of group process. Within the context of this wider circle of acquaintance in which her attachments were less developed, Samantha experienced an intense, irrational anxiety. She tried to compensate for this by desperately attempting to raise her status within the group, unfortunately using Julia as her fall guy. At the time, Samantha was not conscious of what she was doing or why. However, the group had affected her so power-fully that even her protective instincts toward her best friend had been temporarily overruled.

Bion suggests that all groups churn up primitive, unconscious fantasies. Even placid, mild-mannered children can get caught up in a pack mentality at times.

I'm not saying that all experiences driven by group processes are bad. Far from it—some of your child's best moments will likely be provided by groups: They can foster moments of ten-der intimacy, invincible solidarity, and can bring out some of our best qualities. However, children should be helped to understand that groups can trigger unusual behavior in others and that they can arouse passions in them that need to be managed responsibly. To some degree, at least, forewarned is forearmed.

Scapegoating

In Old Testament Israel, a priest would lay hands on a goat and symbolically invest the animal with the sins of the community. The unfortunate goat was then chased out beyond the city wall, in theory carrying the guilt of the city away with it. These days, the phrase *scapegoating* refers to a particularly unpleasant but commonplace group process that causes many children a great deal of misery.

Groups have a horrible habit of electing one or more members to serve as a convenient bin for the disposal of the group's fears and anxieties. In a case of "Better him than me," it seems that groups often deal with collective fears about being picked on or thrown out by ostracizing one or more of their own members. For the spectators, the bad thing is happening to someone else, and for a while, at least, this makes everyone else feel a little less on edge.

New group leaders often establish their dominance by casting someone into the role of scapegoat. This also allows them to buy the favor of the group by temporarily soothing everyone's hidden anxieties. However, for the child to whom this is happening, the experience of scapegoating can be horrible, particularly because it is often unclear why an individual is being singled out.

Your child needs to be able to recognize scapegoating when it happens and take a firm stand when she encounters it. If she is already using the assertiveness skills outlined in this chapter, it is far less likely that she will be picked on. However, be aware that insecure children vying for high status within the group might feel threatened by an assertive child and be on the lookout for opportunities to declaw a potential rival.

Scapegoating is bullying and needs to be dealt with swiftly and robustly. A child who understands the principle of scapegoating is more likely to spot it in the early stages and take action before it gets out of hand—whether he is the scapegoat or whether he observes the signs that someone else is being positioned in that role. Common signs that scapegoating is taking place include these:

➤ The potential victim becomes the subject of gossip.

➤ The level of "good-natured" teasing around the potential scapegoat increases.

➤ Members of the group might express pseudoconcern about the potential victim and come together either formally or informally to discuss what to do about the "problem" group member.

➤ New allegiances are formed within the group that are designed to exclude the soon-to-be-scapegoated child. High-status group members might court the scapegoat's existing allies and friends, to lure them away.

➤ The scapegoat discovers that he is not being given information that he needs to participate fully in the group—no one tells him the time of the party, that he needed to bring his swimming things, that fancy dress was no longer required.

This is all ugly and hurtful stuff, but if a child can spot these telltale signs and acts decisively, he can possibly abort scapegoating in its early stages. If the process can be exposed for what it is, group members might come to their senses and be able to regain conscious control. The target victim also must assertively communicate his feelings. It's hard to stick the knife in when you are genuinely in touch with someone's suffering.

Scapegoating operates most powerfully in closed groups that have strong boundaries separating them from the outside world. In William Golding's classic novel *Lord of the Flies*, things get really out of hand among a group of isolated, shipwrecked school children because they lose contact with any frame of reference beyond the tribal society they have created. If your child does see scapegoating occurring, she shouldn't hold back from telling a teacher or other adult. Apart from anything else, an adult's involvement will break the illusion that the group is sealed off from the outside world and help defuse the scapegoating dynamic.

Group Roles

The scapegoat is one role into which groups can cast their members, but there are many others. Rather like a play in which the parts can be filled by different actors, so the drama of group life tends to throw up the same stereotypes time after time. Common roles include the Rebel, the Clown, the Rescuer, the Gate-keeper, and the Conciliator. Each role performs a specialized function for the group, in much the same way that the different physical organs serve the needs of the whole body. What your child needs to recognize is that groups can often cast children into roles that they wouldn't necessarily choose for themselves. The currents of group life can be very hard to swim against.

When his parents moved to a new town, Micah left his junior high school with glowing reports. His teachers regarded him as a charming, responsible, and well-adjusted boy. Micah's sporting ability had made him something of a hero to other children at Midfield Junior High. However, when he joined his new high school, everything changed. Micah never really settled in, and within a few months, his performance in class took a dive. His parents were particularly concerned by reports from Micah's teachers that he had become disruptive in class. Previously a quiet and studious boy, they were now being told that Micah seemed to be drawing attention to himself at every opportunity. If he wasn't deliberately falling off his chair in class, he was playing pranks on the teachers or setting off the fire alarm.

His parents wracked their brains to figure out what was wrong, but there seemed to be no obvious explanation for this uncharacteristic change in Micah's behavior. He didn't appear to be worried or depressed. He had generally coped well with the move and said he liked his new school and the friends he was making there. Concerned that the new friends might be the source of the problem, his parents investigated further. However, according to Micah's teachers, his new social circle consisted of industrious, popular children. In fact, they were pleased to note that he was getting along particularly well with Lewis, the captain of the football team, whose maturity and strong leadership qualities they felt made him an ideal role model.

Ironically, it turned out that Lewis was the crux of the problem. Within his new group of friends, the role that Micah had previously filled in his old school—that of the charismatic leader—was already being filled by Lewis. The group didn't need a new

Hero, but it did have a vacancy for a Clown. The well-behaved, studious circle of friends badly needed someone to express the manic, madcap energy that they had managed to subdue in themselves.

Without consciously choosing the role for himself, Micah had unwittingly put himself forward. His need to fit in and secure a place within the group was driving him to behave in a way that took everyone by surprise, even Micah himself. It was only by making Micah conscious of what was going on that he was able to start rejecting his new group role and establish a less self-destructive identity for himself.

Ages and Stages

Children should also be aware that, just like people, groups go through different stages of development. Entering a group when it is founded is a very different experience from entering a group that has already been established. Bruce Tuckman has divided the life of the small group into five (nearly rhyming) stages: forming, storming, norming, performing, and adjourning.

As the name suggests, during the forming stage, the group comes together. At this point, everyone is feeling their way. Group participants tend to be quite open, trying hard to establish connections with other members. Members strive to find similarities and areas of shared experience that can bind the group together. Hostility is rarely expressed at this stage, and group members concentrate on gathering information about each other. This is quite a stressful phase, and children (and adults) are often not very discriminating about the bonds and alliances they form. There is an opportunistic quality to friendships formed in the early stages of group life that means many of these relationships will either wither or end up being pruned back later on.

The next stage, storming, is more turbulent. At this point, group members start to feel more at ease with one another and often start jockeying for position, status, and power. The storming phase is often accompanied by petty feuds, arguments, and bickering.

Norming is the phase during which the group establishes the rules, principles, and routines by which it will operate. Among children, these rules are often unspoken and invisible—but children who fall foul of them soon know about it. Most groups are pretty conservative and have little tolerance for members who don't play by the established rules or who challenge the status quo.

I remember watching a group of girls happily jumping rope on a school playground some years ago when another child tried to join in. She had a jump rope and her opening gambit was to perform a dazzling series of jumps in front of the other girls. It was an impressive display, but instead of inviting her to join them, the leader of the group fixed a steely eye on the newcomer and announced tartly, "That isn't how *we* do it here."

According to Tuckman, after storming and norming have taken place, the group is in a position to move on with its appointed task (performing) until the day inevitably comes when the group must disband. This is the adjourning stage. Just as the formation stage can be stressful, the disbanding of an established group can evoke deep emotions. If your child is leaving a group that has played a significant part in her life, prepare her for moving on and be sensitive to the strong feelings of loss that children can experience during such endings. Holding a ritual such as a leaving party or even a special family meal to mark the event can give your child a sense of closure and provide an opportunity to come to terms with the changes taking place.

Practice Makes Perfect

This chapter has provided only the briefest introduction to steps you can take to help your child manage his relationships better. However, if your child grasps even some of the principles outlined in these few pages, they can make an enormous difference in the quality of the relationships he forms in life. Where better to learn these skills than within his relationship with you, the parent? Other relationships are much less tolerant, much less forgiving than the one that exists between parent and child. You are ideally placed to provide the sensitive coaching, feedback, and support that your child will need as he comes to grips with the difficult business of getting along with others—and staying in control while he does so.

Quick Summary
Action Points

✎ Help your child understand that anger is a normal and healthy emotion, but one that needs to be controlled.

✎ Make your child familiar with her personal anger "warning signs" and help her act quickly when she spots them using the Traffic Light Rule.

✎ Keep an eye on the motives your child ascribes to others—and any emotionally loaded language he uses to describe situations.

✎ Train your child to become an assertive communicator:

→ Show her how to use "I" statements and appropriate body language to create the right impression.

→ Help your child draw up a personal "Bill of Rights."

→ Teach specific assertiveness techniques such as the broken record and fogging.

→ Practice the skills of assertive negotiation.

✎ Give your child insight into the way operate:

→ Help him understand processes such as scapegoating and know how to deal with them.

→ Make sure she is aware of the way groups can create roles for their members.

→ Support him in dealing with the ages and stages of group life.

SEVEN

Unstoppable:
Boosting Your Child's Problem-Solving Skills

In various studies of resilient children, good emotional control and strong problem-solving skills consistently emerge as two characteristics of children who are better at coping with life. In reality, these two factors are related: Children who don't over-react in a crisis are more likely to retain the presence of mind needed to find a way forward, while children who are confident in their ability to solve problems are less likely to be fazed when difficulties do crop up. Knowing that you can cope in a crisis is half the battle in maintaining self-control when things aren't going according to plan.

In this chapter, we will consider specific problem-solving skills that we can teach children. We also explore the values and attitudes that will enable your child to encounter frustration and disappointment, without letting emotion overwhelm him.

Focusing on Solutions

Some of the problem-solving techniques children often find the most helpful come from a field of counseling called Brief Solution-focused Therapy. The hallmark of this approach is not to get bogged down in "problem-saturated talk," but to concentrate instead on reviewing the occasions when things *do* work out and using your child's existing resources to forge ahead toward solutions.

One tool often used in solution-focused sessions is the so-called "miracle question." How this works is that you ask the person with the problem to imagine precisely how life would be different if the problem was already solved.

You can introduce this by asking your child to imagine that he has a magic wand or some other supernatural means of making the problem disappear. Or you can ask him to picture in detail how things would change if he woke up the next morning and the problem had disappeared overnight. What would he be doing differently? How would people around him be reacting? How would this affect other areas of his life?

Help your child imagine how he would be behaving if he *didn't* feel so jealous of his sister. When he pictures himself as the self-confident person he ideally wants to be, does your son imagine himself still hanging out with the same gang of unruly friends? If the family was currently getting along as well as it did during that blissful summer vacation in Cancun, what behaviors would an observer notice more of, and what would he see less of?

The miracle question is actually a neat device for reframing a problem. By standing it on its head, it defines the original problem in terms of its consequences rather than causes. In doing so, it translates these consequences into a cluster of mini problems, each of which can then be tackled in its own right. Anthony D'Angelo recommends that, when dealing with problems, you should "dig at the roots instead of just hacking at the leaves." In practice, however, addressing the results of their difficulties sometimes enables children to find an accessible way in, whereas trying to tackle the source can feel daunting for them. Sometimes a bit of judicious pruning does the job.

The Wolf in Boy's Clothing

Elliot was driving everyone crazy. He was fighting at school, being constantly rude to teachers, and his mother and father no longer felt able to manage his behavior at home. "He just seems to think he can do what he wants, when he wants ... and if he doesn't get his own way, there's all hell to pay. It's so wearing," confessed his mother, while Elliot glared suspiciously from the corner of the consulting room.

Elliot was a much-wanted only child. Sarah, his mother, had suffered several miscarriages before he was born, and Elliot had also contracted meningitis as a baby. For a while, his parents had thought he might not pull through. Because of these experiences, they had found it very hard to be strict with him and tended to wrap him in bubble wrap. Saying "no" to Elliot was certainly not something that Sarah and Bill were used to.

However, instead of persuading his parents that they needed to take a firmer line with him (which, arguably, they did), the key was to involve Elliot in solving his own problem. The first step was to help him to see that he had a problem to solve. Once alone, we shifted the focus away from the impact his conduct was having on others and began to think together about the ways in which his behavior was affecting his life. What was it like when everyone was shouting at him? Did things feel happy at home? Did the teachers treat him differently from everyone else? How did he feel about that? What did he think would happen if it continued?

Elliot acknowledged that being the Wolf Boy (which was what he called his badly behaved self) did have significant drawbacks as well as advantages. In fact, he knew deep inside that he didn't want to be like that. The problem, as he saw it, was that he often felt really angry when people tried to tell him what to do, and he wasn't sure he could stop. This was where the miracle question came in. I asked Elliot how he thought his life would change if it was possible to wave a magic wand and he just didn't feel that anger inside him anymore.

As Elliot was struggling with this, I asked him to draw a cartoon that showed his life *after* his inner wolf had been removed. Post-lupinectomy, he drew a picture of himself playing happily with his friends on a warm sunny day, another of him sitting attentively in class with his hand up, and a frame of his family all holding hands on an outing to Legoland. The images were bright, colorful, and cheerful. Elliot shook his head dolefully as he put down his pen. "I am not that good boy [pointing to himself in the picture]. I don't feel like him anymore," he said glumly.

"Rather than trying to *feel* like him," I replied, "do you think you might be able to *do* any of the things you've drawn yourself doing in these pictures? If you had to pretend you were this Elliot so no one could tell you were still the Wolf Boy inside, what would you need to do? Can you think of any small changes that might make you look a bit more like him on the outside?"

Together we came up with a list of behaviors Elliot would have to adopt to convince everyone. He would no longer be disruptive in class. He would walk away when other children tried to pick fights with him. He would go to bed on time without the usual drama. He would say "please" and "thank you" instead of demanding and grabbing what he wanted.

Elliot thought this was a hilarious idea—that by simply changing aspects of his behavior, he could "become" someone else. He was also tickled by how stunned and confused everyone would be if he managed it. I explained that it might not be as easy as he thought and he might have to do it a bit at a time, but Elliot was up for the challenge.

Two weeks later, the family came to see me again. Elliot had done himself proud. "He's been a different boy," his mother announced. "School has been asking when the old Elliot is coming back." Later I asked Elliot whether he thought his experiment was working. "Yes," he crowed, "I fooled them all!" Then his tone became accusing. "But you played a trick on me...because when I stopped being Wolf Boy on the outside, I didn't feel so much like him on the inside anymore." "Really?" I asked innocently, "and which do you like better?" Elliot rolled his eyes and said nothing. But two months later, the Wolf Boy was still nowhere to be seen.

Sometimes, as Elliot's story illustrates, helping a child shift attention away from the cause of the problem and refocus on what the resolution would look like can point the way to a solution. Many children learn best by doing, so being able to break down a problem into manageable, practical steps often appeals to them. Looking at the end state after the problem has gone away can help clarify precisely what steps need to be taken.

Ask your children what they would do, how things would be, if they could wave a magic wand? Offer them the chance to draw if that helps. Then help break it down into small, practical actions.

Using Creative Visualization to Support Problem Solving

Children know a lot more than they think they do and are potentially far better at solving all sorts of problems than many adults give them credit for. Unfortunately, our society often sends them the message that they are "just kids" and teaches them that they stand little chance of arriving at workable solutions without adult help. Consequently, they often doubt their own capabilities.

Paradoxically, children can sometimes be empowered by allowing them to disown their abilities as problem solvers. Helping them create scenarios in which answers and solutions are provided by figures "outside" themselves can actually enable them to tap into their considerable problem-solving resources.

One way children can learn to do this is through guided visualization. In their imaginations, children can be encouraged to consult sources of wisdom for answers and strategies needed to tackle the unresolved situations and difficulties they may be facing.

With children under the age of seven, you can try using the story of the Wise King. Ask the child to imagine herself making a journey through a magical forest with the problem in her backpack. The problem is usually uncomfortable to carry, and (maybe a bit sadistically) I suggest that the journey is long and hard. At various points along the way, introduce your child to different characters dwelling in the forest. As the child meets various animals—the boy playing by the stream, the old woman baking bread, and so on—she asks each of them for help with her problem but always gets the same reply: "I cannot help you. But I know who can. You need to find the Wise King (or Queen). He is very old and very wise and can surely help you."

If you are feeling inventive, each character can provide an example of a problem the Wise King has solved—how he taught the blackbird to fly, the old woman to put yeast in the bread to make it rise, the boy to stop people from stealing his candy, and so on. As with all these visualization exercises, the elements of repetition and vivid sensual detail help lull your child into a relaxed receptive state. Most children relish the storytelling element of this technique, and you can even get them to contribute their own suggestions at this point—a process that can help prime a problem-solving mindset.

Eventually, the child comes to a clearing in the forest and spies a magnificent castle. The drawbridge is lowered and the child is greeted by a steward who says the king is expecting her. The child is given audience with the king, who looks appropriately wise and all-knowing. ("His eyes are the very deepest, purest blue, like a pool so deep you could never reach the bottom even if you could hold your breath for a whole day....") The child unwraps the problem and presents it to the Wise King, who inspects it carefully and gives it due regal consideration.

You then ask your child to imagine that the king is beckoning her forward and whispering something in her ear so quietly that only she can hear. You could also ask the child to picture the king giving her a gift to help with the problem. The audience with the king ends, the visualization is wrapped up, and the child is gently reoriented to the real world.

When the exercise is over, feel free to ask your child what the Wise King whispered in her ear or what symbolic gift she was given. Occasionally, a child will tell you that he didn't really say anything. In this case, you nod sagely and say that because the king is so old, he sometimes whispers so quietly that it can be very hard to hear him at first, but she might remember what he said later. However, you will often be amazed at the maturity and creativity of some of the king's advice.

One young girl, Janine, whose brother had suddenly started being mean to her, told me gravely that the Wise King had given her a key. When she used this key to unlock her brother's heart and look inside, she discovered he was feeling "very afraid." Instead of fighting with him anymore, she needed to be more understanding. She would tell Spike "not to be scared," even though she didn't know exactly what was frightening him.

Her mother later told me that that the brother was scheduled for a potentially painful medical investigation. It was certainly plausible that Spike's changed behavior toward his sister had been brought on by underlying anxiety about this. As we saw in Chapter 5, "Wrestling with Monsters: Overcoming Stress and Anxiety," aggression can often be brought on by anxiety, and this is exactly what Janine's intuition was telling her.

Another variation of this technique is widely practiced in neurolinguistic programming. Ask your child to picture someone he really admires or looks up to—a sporting legend, a film star, or maybe even a relative. Get your child to imagine the hero figure in an appropriate setting, and encourage him to put himself in his hero's shoes so that he has a clear sense of what the person feels like and what the world looks like through his or her eyes.

Now ask your child, still in the guise of the hero figure, to step into the problem situation. What does he think about it? How would he handle it? What sort of strategies would he adopt? Seeing the problem from the perspective of someone they already regard as resourceful and competent can help children analyze the situation in different ways and generate innovative and helpful solutions for themselves.

Using an imaginary "somebody else" to solve your children's problems is a useful way of helping them find their own answers.

Map It Out

Edward Hodnett claims, "A question asked in the right way often points to its own answer." The same is true of many problems and difficulties children routinely face. If children can learn to formulate their difficulties in the right way, they are usually more than halfway down the path toward a solution. However, children often present difficulties without key aspects of problem solving: both seeing the bigger picture and breaking down the issue into its component parts, detecting similarities between the structure of old problems and new ones, and appreciating which of the skills and resources they already have might be relevant.

One tool that can help children overcome these limitations is mind-mapping, a technique pioneered by Tony Buzan in the 1970s. Mind-mapping is now widely used in classroom settings to help children learn and remember academic material. However, it is also invaluable in supporting and nurturing children's problem-solving abilities.

The principles behind mind-mapping are simple. The map creates a visual image of a subject area that exploits the way the brain encodes information as a network of cascading associations. The average human brain consists of approximately 100 billion neurons, and each individual neuron has connections with hundreds or possibly even thousands of others. Depending on the strength of these individual connections, when one neuron fires, it automatically triggers other linked neurons to fire in turn, causing a wave of "spreading activation" across the network.

Mind-mapping mirrors this process on paper. The target subject is represented as a single idea in the middle of a blank piece of paper. From this central hub, the mind-mapper draws out branches representing any new ideas inspired by the original concept. Each of these new ideas can give rise to further associations that are incorporated into the diagram as a network of subbranches. By freely associating in this way, the mind-mapper is quickly able to create an overview of what she already knows and of what information she might still need to gather. By using arrows to draw connections between areas and concepts on the map, the individual is also able to see how different aspects of the subject relate to one another.

The process often sparks new insights. Traditional, logical analysis tends to narrow things down, but in mind-mapping, fresh associations from each node can trigger material that encourages the mind to play freely with ideas. As the connections proliferate, the mind-mapper can link up different areas of the map in unexpected new ways. In short, the mind map is a great tool for helping children think creatively about a wide range of situations.

Before moving on to demonstrate how mind-mapping can help children solve problems, here are just a few of Buzan's general pointers, to help your child get the most out of the mind-mapping process:

1. Use images as well as words. Images stimulate the brain in ways that words don't, and many children are visual thinkers. By combining words and images, Buzan argues that both left- and right-brain hemispheres are engaged, thereby bringing more brain power to the issue.

2. Use color. Again, the brighter and more visually interesting your map becomes, the more likely it is to engage the mapper's attention and creative powers.

3. Use only single words on each branch. When words are paired together, you restrict the range of associations that individual words and concepts might trigger.

4. Try not to censor associations. Productive avenues of thought may come from branches that do not seem immediately relevant. Encourage your child to associate freely.

Techniques such as mind-mapping can help an older child to think through the reasons behind a problem, and therefore bring possible solutions to the surface.

Late Again

In the De Lacey household, the day was not getting off to a good start. Kyan (age nine) was constantly late for school. For some reason, it was proving virtually impossible to get him and his brother, Conrad, out the door in enough time to make it to school. Kyan was getting into trouble with his teachers, his mother was tearing her hair out, and everyone—even Kyan—realized that something needed to change.

Instead of trying to sort out the problem for him, Kyan's parents encouraged him to mind-map the problem for himself first before they sat down and talked about it together that evening. They knew from experience that this was a good way to get Kyan to take ownership of the problem, think about its various elements, and start to work his way toward possible solutions. The map Kyan came up with is re-created here.

When Kyan and his parents looked at Kyan's map together, a number of things became clear. By using this technique to structure his problem, Kyan had been able to explore it in some

detail and make some important connections between different elements.

One thing Kyan learned was that his lateness appeared to be
the result of a number of different factors. These included his
forgetfulness, his last-minute approach, and the trouble he
experienced getting going in the mornings because he was so
tired. However, the mapping process also highlighted how certain elements had a domino effect on each other, keeping the
problem going.

For example, the fact that his exasperated mother was getting
so irate every morning was putting Kyan under so much stress
that it was actually becoming harder for him to concentrate
and remember all the things he needed to do. Also, if he did get
up late, the fact that other members of his family needed to
use the bathroom created an additional delay, so the map
revealed that sleeping in was not an option.

Another helpful aspect of doing the map was that it got Kyan
thinking about contrasting situations in which he was *never*
late. In doing so he was able to identify some of the strategies
responsible. Getting his soccer gear ready the night before and
borrowing his brother's cell phone so he could set an alarm
instead of relying on the defunct clock by his bedside were just
two steps that helped Kyan to always be among the first at his
weekly soccer practice. Kyan realized that he needed to trans-
fer some of these strategies to weekday mornings.

Thinking about all the different things he needed to do to get
ready on school days made Kyan appreciate that he needed a
plan. He couldn't afford to fumble his way through his morning
routine in such a piecemeal, chaotic fashion. At Kyan's suggestion, his parents agreed to write him a checklist on a white
board by the door so that he could do his various tasks in a
sensible order and check them off when he completed them.

However, the most valuable aspect of the mapping process was that it revealed an important dimension of the problem that no one had fully appreciated. It was certainly true that Kyan was tired in the mornings, but mind-mapping helped him understand why. Yes, he was staying up far too late watching TV, and his parents realized that letting the boys have a television in their room wasn't the smartest idea. But the reason for Kyan's late-night viewing was that he had been trying to keep himself awake because of the increasingly anxious thoughts and nightmares he had been having.

This was the crux of the issue—Kyan's sluggish behavior in the morning was ultimately a result of his anxious state of mind. Kyan and his parents now realized that they had a very different problem on their hands. Being late for school was just a symptom; the mind-mapping process helped Kyan identify this. A new set of priorities was clarified, and Kyan's parents were then able to support their son in tackling the source of the problem.

Thinking About Thinking

Have you ever noticed the different ways children approach tasks? In the basement of our local Science Museum, you will find, among other things, a selection of three-dimensional puzzles. Last time we were there, I watched a group of children trying to put them together.

Some children displayed a remarkable urgency, shoving the pieces together in random combinations again and again, obviously hoping that the puzzle would somehow fall into place under their fingers. Needless to say, this strategy wasn't very successful. Most children who used this approach got nowhere and gave up after a few minutes. These children knew their internal clock was ticking. Their desperate manipulations became ever more frantic as their rising frustration became intolerable. Some of these kids ended up dropping the puzzle as if it was red hot or angrily scattering the pieces before rushing on to the next attraction.

Other children started the task in much the same way, manipulating the pieces and trying out different combinations. However, these children were much slower and more deliberate about the process. Every now and again these children paused and examined what they had done. Sometimes they retraced their steps and undid bits of the puzzle they had already assembled. Occasionally, they just picked up a piece and studied it carefully for a few seconds. When they found a combination that seemed to work, this became part of a construction sequence that they deliberately repeated. It was obvious that these children were very aware of what they were doing and were learning as they went along. Sometimes they could be heard muttering under their breath, "This piece can't go here because then that piece won't fit." Most of these children eventually reached a point of sudden clarity, a "eureka" moment, after which they quickly and assuredly assembled the puzzle in a few precise movements.

There are some fascinating contrasts between the approaches of these two groups. Both point to the chicken-and-egg nature of the relationship between the ability to keep emotions in check and the capacity to use suitable mental strategies for getting the job done. The fact that children in the first group couldn't handle their frustration made it very hard for them to think straight. For children in the second group, it was their confidence in tried-and-trusted techniques for working things out and their self-aware learning style that enabled them to stay calm. The same principles apply in many everyday situations.

Being conscious of *how* we achieve results, and being able to review and monitor our progress, has turned out to be a cornerstone of effective learning. In more progressive educational circles, a group of teachers and researchers has been highlighting the importance of *metacognition*, or the ability to think about thinking. These skills come naturally to bright students (or maybe this group has become bright simply because they have always used them), but the good news for the rest of us is that we can cultivate them.

Gifted Kids or Gifted Mothers?

In a fascinating study in the early 1990s, Ellen Moss and her colleagues compared the way that mothers of exceptionally gifted preschoolers talked to them during problem-solving tasks with conversations between a control group of mothers and children with only average scores on a standard IQ test. Having analyzed the strategies the mothers were using, Moss discovered that the mothers of the gifted children were far more likely to be prompting metacognitive strategies than the mothers of the nongifted students.

These strategies included predicting consequences and thinking about the effect of future actions ("Will this piece fit in that space?"), checking results ("Is that right?"), and reality testing or making meaningful comparisons with what was already known ("Should you use such *small* blocks for the foundation?"). Moss also noted that the mothers in the nongifted group spent more time actively directing their children back to the task, while the gifted children's mothers used activity monitoring—their comments helped their children judge for themselves what kind of progress they were making toward their goal.

Moss speculates whether the giftedness of these children had as much to do with the way their parents were relating to them as with any superior level of inborn intelligence. We cannot be sure. But we do know that among populations of school-age children and students, the direct teaching of thinking skills has been shown time and again to produce substantial improvement in academic performance.

Stretch Your Child's Brain Power

Obviously, the level at which these skills can be taught will depend to some extent on the age of your child. During the preschool period, one of the ways parents can support the development of their child's thinking is to point out the features of objects that a child might not spontaneously attend to. And although children ages three and four are usually quite capable of following a sequence of simple steps toward a goal, they can find it much harder to hold the bigger picture in mind and keep that end goal in sight. Reminding them of what they are trying to achieve and refreshing their memory about rules or principles that govern the task can be really useful. Having said this, several researchers believe that between the ages of three and five, most children become able to start reflecting on their experience and are therefore ready to start developing key skills such as predicting, checking results, self-monitoring, and reality testing.

To develop your own child's thinking skills following pointers may be helpful:

> Do tasks that enable you to think together with your child. Make sure you are thinking out loud: "What do we need to do next?" "Is what we're doing now similar to any other problem we have solved in the past?" "Let's pause and consider how we're doing for a moment." "What are we trying to do here?" "Can we do anything to help us make better progress?"

> Always start by helping your child recap what she already knows about a subject or problem so that she can make relevant links and connections and give the task a context. Mind maps are great for this.

> Help your child formulate a plan that will enable him to reach the end goal in a series of productive steps. How will he tackle the task at hand? What obstacles might he encounter? How will he deal with them?

> Foster the four key metacognitive skills: anticipate, check, monitor, and evaluate.

> Help your child see why mastering a particular problem or skill is relevant to her life and how what she is learning ties in with what she already knows.

➤ Always encourage your child to evaluate his *own* performance. What was hard about the task? What helped? What has he learned about approaching similar tasks in future?

➤ As a general rule, ask questions to support or provoke your child's thinking instead of issuing directions or providing easy answers. Olympic medalist and coach David Hemery observes, "If our questions generate more of their awareness and self-responsibility, the likely result is an increase in our young people's self-belief."

➤ Encourage your child to talk to herself as she tackles a task so that she becomes more aware of her own thought processes.

➤ Be careful not to prompt excessively. Children learn best when they can figure something out for themselves. If you are too quick with a helpful question or reminder, they will become reliant on you to do the thinking for them.

➤ Persuade your child not to rush. Self-awareness, monitoring, and in-depth reflection cannot happen if your child is always in a hurry to get to the end. He is also much more likely to make careless mistakes. Model good habits and demonstrate that sometimes it is important to take your time if you really want to understand something properly.

➤ Finally, always help your child to identify and explicitly label any principles, strategies, or rules that are aiding her performance during the task. This enables your child to build up a repertoire of problem-solving skills. Foster the mindset of French mathematician and philosopher René Descartes, who remarked, "Each problem that I solved became a rule which served afterward to solve other problems." Children often deduce and apply principles without being conscious that they are doing so, making them less likely to be able to use them in other situations.

Programmed for Success

So far in this chapter we have focused mainly on improving thinking skills for effective problem solving. However, people who are good at solving problems and who cope well with setbacks do so not just because they possess certain skills, but because they share certain values. Being able to navigate difficulties and dilemmas without losing your cool is ultimately as much a question of attitude as it is of competence. To help children become truly skilled problem solvers, we need to equip them not only with tools and strategies, but also with values to enhance their problem-solving skills.

Researchers studying self-regulation have discovered that people stand a much greater chance of staying in control when they have planned in advance how they will handle difficult situations. Having established protocols already in their heads has been shown to help alcoholics deal better with the temptation to drink and agoraphobics to ward off panic attacks. The values that follow perform a similar job: They support reliable approach strategies that can keep your child grounded while she explores unfamiliar or emotionally hazardous terrain.

What Can I Learn Here?

One of the most distinctive qualities of world-class problem solvers is the ability to embrace mistakes and setbacks as a valuable aspect of the learning process. The irrepressible Thomas Edison, whose many inventions brought electric light and power into modern homes, was coming from precisely this position when he stated dogmatically, "I haven't failed. I've found 10,000 ways that don't work." We need to help our children understand that the problems that initially defeat them are the very ones that have the most to offer them in terms of their personal growth. As Nobel Prize–winning physicist Frank Wilczek put it, "If you don't make mistakes, you're not working on hard enough problems. And that's a big mistake."

Psychologist Carol Dweck claims that our defensive attitude toward failure is often linked to what she calls the "fixed" mindset. People with such a mindset tend to see ability as a fixed commodity, predetermined at birth. From such a perspective, failure is always intimidating because our errors disclose to us, and everyone else, the limits of our talent. They dictate whether we are intelligent or stupid, competent or inept, winners or losers. Children with a fixed mindset constantly compare themselves with others in order to locate themselves on a perceived scale of achievement. Consequently, they tend to focus purely on getting results rather than allowing themselves to engage fully in the process of discovery. They also tend to play it safe rather than risk the humiliation of failure.

By contrast, Dweck observes that children with a "growth" mindset seemed to positively relish problems that extended and baffled them. Seen through their eyes, these problems were the ones that provided opportunities for development and could really teach them something. Puzzles that were too easy couldn't do that. These children instinctively believed that far from being fixed, their ability was flexible and could be expanded, but only by constantly pushing their existing boundaries and making sense of their mistakes.

Encourage your child to make friends with failure and respect what it can offer. Help her cultivate the attitude of great American administrator and academic John Gardner, who claimed, "We are continually faced with a series of great opportunities brilliantly disguised as insoluble problems." Celebrate the hard-won victories instead of the easy ones, and help your child mine insights from setbacks in an optimistic and nonjudgmental fashion.

> Raise your child to believe that a difficult problem is an exciting prospect and that failure is a step on the path to success.

Stick with It

"Kids, you tried your best and failed miserably. The lesson is, never try."
—Homer Simpson

Homer's advice to Lisa and Bart is amusing because it stands on its head of one of the basic principles of achievement in any field of endeavor. Perseverance far outstrips talent when it comes to deciding who will ultimately master a challenge or overcome an obstacle in life. Calvin Coolidge was right when he said, "The slogan 'Press On' has solved, and always will solve, the problems of the human race," but helping children develop this kind of stamina is no easy matter.

The pace of the modern world conditions our children to expect everything instantly. Microwaves produce steaming-hot meals in a matter of seconds, Internet shopping brings goods from all over the world to our door, and most children play computer games that deliver a rapid succession of satisfying "hits" in return for very little sustained effort. One drawback of this is that today's children often have very little experience in the benefits of perseverance. They have never had opportunities to prove to themselves that it can be worthwhile to tolerate frustration and to press through unyielding circumstances. For such kids, Homer's advice seems eminently sensible.

Not only should you stress the importance of keeping going when things get tough, but you should also ensure that your child is involved in mastering at least one skill that delivers results in proportion to the sustained effort invested in it. Examples include playing a musical instrument or learning to paint or draw. Maybe your child has a sporting talent that can be developed. It doesn't matter what it is but, if your child is to hold it together and persevere when she encounters problems, she will need evidence that resisting the urge to give up can be worthwhile.

Find a hobby or sport that your child wants to do but that requires perseverance, and encourage him to stick with it.

Don't Go It Alone

When we think of inventors, we usually conjure up an image of some eccentric Professor Branestrawm figure alone in his workshop. The reality of effective problem solving is very different. Edison didn't invent his famous light bulb on his own. While testing out more than 3,000 different materials to find a suitable filament, he employed a whole team of research assistants. Einstein used to bounce his latest relativity theories off his physicist wife, Mileva Maric, and, at the turn of the nineteenth century, Marie Curie made her pioneering discoveries into radioactivity in collaboration with her husband, Pierre.

Help your children to appreciate that intelligent problem solving often means involving other people and making the most of their knowledge and experience. Simply having to communicate the issues to someone else requires them to begin organizing their ideas, and having someone on hand to act as a sounding board can also help them evaluate possible solutions.

Encourage your child to share his problems with you, but when he does, try to resist the temptation to "take over" and deliver a solution. It will be far more helpful for your child in the long run if you can support and nurture his own problem-solving potential by giving constructive feedback on his efforts to find a way forward.

Never Assume

In 1986, when the space shuttle *Challenger* exploded in a ball of flame 73 seconds after lift-off, the U.S. government commissioned a thorough investigation into the causes of the accident. A key figure in the investigation was Professor Richard Feynman, one of the most original and incisive minds of his generation. What Feynman's investigations revealed was shocking: Managers at NASA had pushed ahead with the launch despite warnings from the technical team that the O-ring seals on the solid rocket boosters were potentially faulty and that the cold weather might cause significant problems for the shuttle. The managers simply assumed that everything would go smoothly. They saw only what they wanted to see, even though the people who knew best were telling them that their analysis of the situation was skewed. The result was the unnecessary death of seven astronauts.

Outstanding problem solvers are often the people who challenge the assumptions everyone else takes for granted. They take account of all the information they have at their disposal, not just the bits that fit with their existing model of the world. They do not rely on hearsay or second-hand knowledge when it contradicts the evidence of their own observations or powers of reasoning.

Feynman wrote how grateful he was to his father for teaching him how to make careful observations of the natural world, unclouded by preconceptions about what he would see. Leonardo da Vinci's outstanding scientific and artistic genius also found a common root in his capacity to look at what was in front of him without being impaired by conventional wisdom.

By "thinking outside the box," these individuals were able to see the true nature of things more clearly and develop some impressively innovative solutions. This is an invaluable quality for good problem solvers to possess because, as Einstein dryly pointed out, "The significant problems we have cannot be solved at the same level of thinking with which we created them." On a practical level, if what your child is doing currently isn't working, encourage him to try something else!

> Encourage children to question everything, challenge assumptions, think about problems in different ways, and be creative.
>
>

Also train your children to feel at ease with uncertainty. In a televised interview, Richard Feynman emphasized the importance for good scientists to be comfortable with doubt and "not knowing." The same applies to budding problem solvers. Teach your children to think through situations for themselves and ensure that they are taking into account all the relevant facts. Rushing to a half-baked solution is seldom a productive way to proceed. Encourage your children to question everything and hold all "certainties" lightly. In doing so, you will encourage flexible thinking that will produce creative responses to even the most difficult challenges life presents.

Quick Summary
Action Points

🐟 Encourage your child to focus on solutions using techniques such as answering the "miracle question" and reframing complex problems in manageable terms.

🐟 Help your child tap into her own problem-solving powers by enabling her to recruit "outside" help in the form of an imaginary mentor.

🐟 Teach your child how to explore and structure problems using tools such as mind-mapping.

🐟 Train your child to become aware of the processes that underlie productive thinking and successful problem solving:

→ Think aloud with your child.

→ Develop the four key skills: anticipate, check, monitor, and evaluate.

→ Ask questions that enable your child to find his own solutions.

🐟 Help your child take note of the strategies that work.

🐟 Cultivate the mindset and values of world-class problem solvers: perseverance, collaboration, open-mindedness, and curiosity.

And Finally...Happily Ever After?

> "Feelings are real and legitimate; children behave and misbehave for a reason, even if adults cannot figure it out."
> —Author unknown

I wrote this book with three goals in mind. The first was to try and help parents understand the reasons why children misbehave and urge you to keep grappling with the underlying causes. Despite what you may have seen on television, when it comes to successful parenting, there are no quick fixes.

Second, I wanted to make the point that the skirmishes we have with our offspring pale in insignificance compared with the internal battles our children are waging against their own feelings and impulses. Although the landscape of childhood can feel alien to grown-ups at times, we need to understand the minds and hearts of our children if we are to become useful allies in their battle for self-control.

Finally, I hoped to convince you that we are long overdue for a shift in the parenting agenda. We need to set our sights beyond the management of children's behavior and embrace the broader opportunities and privileges that parenthood offers. This book tries to map out a wider definition of parental "discipline" and acknowledge our duty to equip children with the psychological skills they need to behave well—and, more importantly, to live well.

Only you can judge how well these goals have been achieved. Nevertheless, we should probably all pay heed to the words of Jackie Onassis: "If you bungle raising your children, I don't think whatever else you do well matters very much." It is tough, then, that parenting well turns out to be such a demanding business. I certainly can't afford to put myself on any pedestal as a parent (as my wife and sons will be quick to tell you), and I am often just as beleaguered as the next struggling dad. However, working as a psychologist has given me some faith in the transformations that can be achieved if children are equipped with the tools they need to begin mastering their emotional lives.

I trust that you will feel inspired to try out the techniques described in these pages for yourself and, at the very least, that the journey will bring you and your child closer. G. K. Chesterton remarked that he liked children "if they're properly cooked." My hope is that in these pages, you have found some recipes that will be useful to you both along the way.

References and Further Reading

Bandura, A. "Self-Efficacy: Toward a Unifying Theory of Behavior Change." *Psychological Review* 84 (1977): 191–215.

Baumeister, R. F. "Esteem Threat, Self-Regulatory Breakdown, and Emotional Distress as Factors in Self-Defeating Behavior." *Review of General Psychology* 1 (1997): 145–174.

Baumeister, R. F., E. Bratslavsky, M. Muraven, and D. M. Tice. "Ego Depletion: Is the Active Self a Limited Resource?" *Journal of Personality and Social Psychology* 74 (1998): 1252–1265.

Baumeister, R. F., and K. D. Vohs. *Handbook of Self-Regulation—Research, Theory, and Applications*. London: The Guilford Press, 2004.

Berk, L. E., and A. Winsler. 1995. *Scaffolding Children's Learning: Vygotsky and Early Childhood Education*. National Association for the Education of Young Children, Washington, D.C. ERIC, ED 384443.

Bourne, E. J. *The Anxiety and Phobia Workbook*. Oakland, CA: New Harbinger Publications, 2005.

Bransford, J. D., A. L. Brown, and R. Cocking (eds.). *How People Learn*. Washington, D.C.: National Academy Press: 2000.

Brown, A. L. "Metacognition, Executive Control, Self-Regulation, and Other More Mysterious Mechanisms," in *Metacognition, Motivation and Understanding*, edited by F. E. Weinert and R. H. Kluwe. New Jersey: Lawrence Erlbaum Associates, 1987.

Butler, G. *Overcoming Social Anxiety and Shyness: A Self-Help Guide Using Cognitive Behavioral Techniques*. London: Robinson, 1999.

Buzan, Tony. *Mind Maps for Kids: An Introduction*. London: Thorsons, 2003.

Coleman, J. C., and L. B. Hendry. *The Nature of Adolescence*. 3rd ed. London: Routledge, 1999.

Dapretto, M. "Understanding Emotions in Others: Mirror Neuron Dysfunction in Children with Autism Spectrum Disorders." *Nature Neuroscience* 9, no. 1 (2006): 28–30.

Davies, W. *Overcoming Anger and Irritability*. New York: New York University Press, 2000.

Day, J. *Creative Visualization with Children*. Shaftesbury, England: Element Books, 1994.

De Bono, E. *Teach Your Child How to Think*. London: Penguin Books, 1993.

Doyle Gentry, W. *Anger Management for Dummies*. New Jersey: Wiley, 2007.

Dweck, C. *Mindset: The New Psychology of Success*. New York: Random House, 2006.

Dweck, C. S. *Self-Theories: Their Role in Motivation, Personality, and Development*. Philadelphia: Taylor and Francis, 1999.

Edwards, D. *My Naughty Little Sister's Friends*. London: Egmont, 1962.

Eisenberg, N., R. Lennon, and K. Roth. "Pro-social Development: A Longitudinal Study." *Developmental Psychology* 19, no. 6 (1983): 846–855.

Faber, A., and E. Mazlish. *How to Talk So Kids Will Listen and Listen So Kids Will Talk*. New York: HarperCollins, 2002.

Fennell, M. *Overcoming Low Self-Esteem*. London: Robinson, 1999.

Feynman, R. P. *Surely You're Joking, Mr. Feynman! Adventures of a Curious Character*. London: Vantage, 1992.

Friedberg, R. D., and J. M. McClure. *Clinical Practice of Cognitive Therapy with Children and Adolescents—The Nuts and Bolts*. London: The Guilford Press, 2002.

Gallo, D. "Educating for Empathy, Reason and Imagination." *The Journal of Creative Behavior* 23, no. 2 (1989): 98–115.

Goleman, D. *Emotional Intelligence: Why It Can Matter More Than IQ*. London: Bloomsbury, 1996.

Greenberger, D., and C. A. Padesky. *Mind Over Mood: Change How You Feel By Changing the Way You Think*. New York: The Guilford Press, 1995.

Hargie, O., and D. Dickson. *Skilled Interpersonal Communication: Research, Theory and Practice*. 4th ed. London: Routledge, 2004.

Hartley, M. *The Assertiveness Handbook*. London: Sheldon Press, 2005.

Hawton, K., P. M. Salkovskis, J. Kirk, and D. M. Clark. *Cognitive Behavior Therapy for Psychiatric Problems—A Practical Guide.* Oxford: Oxford University Press, 1989.

Hemery, D. *How to Help Children Find the Champion Within Themselves.* London: BBC Worldwide, 2005.

Henley, M. *Teaching Self-Control: A Curriculum for Responsible Behavior.* Bloomington, IN: National Education Service, 2003.

Higgins, S., E. Hall, V. Baumfield, and D. Moseley. "A Meta-Analysis of the Impact of the Implementation of Thinking Skills Approaches on Pupils," in *Research Evidence,* in Education Library, EPPI-Centre, Social Science Research Unit, Institute of Education, University of London, 2005.

Iannotti, R. J. "Effect of Role-Taking Experiences on Role Taking, Empathy, Altruism, and Aggression." *Developmental Psychology* 14, no. 2 (1978): 119–124.

Lezak, M. D. *Neuropsychological Assessment.* 3rd ed. Oxford: Oxford University Press, 1995.

Lucas, B., and A. Smith. *Help Your Child to Succeed: The Essential Guide for Parents.* Stafford, UK: Network Educational Press Ltd., 2002.

Malan, D. H. *Individual Psychotherapy and the Science of Pyschodynamics.* 2nd ed. Oxford: Butterworth Heinemann, 1997.

Maslow, A. H. *Toward a Psychology of Being.* 2nd ed. New York: Van Nostrand Reinhold, 1968.

McMullin, R. E. *The New Handbook of Cognitive Therapy Techniques.* New York: Norton, 2000.

Mills, R. S., and J. E. Grusec. "Cognitive, Affective, and Behavioral Consequences of Praising Altruism." *Merrill-Palmer Quarterly* 35, no. 3 (1989): 299–326.

Mischel, W. "Processes in Delay Gratification," in *Advances in Experimental Social Psychology*, edited by L. Berkowitz. San Diego: C. A. Academic Press, 1974.

Mischel, W., Y. Shoda, and M. I. Rodriguez. "Delay of Gratification in Children." *Science* 244, no. 4907 (1989): 933–938.

Moore, B. E., and B. D. Fine (eds.). *Psycho-Analysis: The Major Concepts.* London: Yale University Press, 1995.

Moss, E. S., and F. F. Strayer. "Interactive Problem-Solving of Mothers and Gifted and Nongifted Preschoolers." *International Journal of Behavioral Development* 13, no. 2 (1990): 177–197.

Nettle, D. *Personality: What Makes You the Way You Are.* Oxford: Oxford University Press, 2007.

Payne, R. A. *Relaxation Techniques: A Practical Handbook for the Healthcare Professional.* Edinburg: Churchill Livingstone, 2002.

Rizzolatti, G., and L. Graighero. "The Mirror-Neuron System." *Annual Review of Neuroscience* 2204, no. 27 (2004): 169–92.

Sax, L. *Why Gender Matters: What Parents and Teachers Need to Know About the Emerging Science of Sex Differences.* London: Doubleday, 2005.

Segal, Z. V., J. M. G. Williams, and J. D. Teasdale. *Mindfulness-Based Cognitive Therapy for Depression: A New Approach to Preventing Relapse.* New York: The Guilford Press, 2002.

Selekman, M. D. *Pathways to Change: Brief Therapy Solutions with Difficult Adolescents.* London: The Guilford Press, 1993.

Selekman, M. D. *Solution-Focused Therapy with Children: Harnessing Family Strengths for Systemic Change.* London: The Guilford Press, 1997.

Seligman, M. *The Optimistic Child: Proven Program to Safeguard Children from Depression and Build Lifelong Resilience.* New York: Harper Collins, 1995.

Shuster, C. "Emotions Count: Scaffolding Children's Representations of Themselves and Their Feelings to Develop Emotional Intelligence," in *Issues in Early Childhood Education: Curriculum, Teacher Education, and Dissemination of Information.* Proceedings of the Lilian Katz Symposium (Champaign, IL, November 5–7, 2000).

Smith, C., and D. Nylund. *Narrative Therapies with Children and Adolescents.* London: The Guilford Press, 1997.

Staricoff, M., and A. Rees. *Start Thinking: Daily Starters to Inspire Thinking in Primary Classrooms.* Birmingham: Imaginative Minds, 2005.

Stern, D. N. *The Interpersonal World of the Infant: A View from Psychoanalysis and Developmental Psychology.* New York: Basic Books, 1985.

Stiles, J. "Neural Plasticity and Cognitive Development." *Developmental Neuropsychology* 18, no. 2 (2000): 237–272.

Tangney, J. P., R. F. Baumeister, and A. Boone. "High Self-Control Predicts Good Adjustment, Less Pathology, Better Grades, and Interpersonal Success." *Journal of Personality* 72 (2004): 271–324.

Tice, D. M., E. Bratslavsky, and R. Baumeister. "Emotional Distress Regulation Takes Precedence Over Impulse Control: If You Feel Bad, Do It!" *Journal of Personality and Social Psychology* 80, no. 1 (2001): 53–67.

Travers, P. L. *Mary Poppins.* London: HarperCollins, 1934.

Valiente, C., N. Eisenberg, R. A. Fabes, S. A. Shepard, A. Cumberland, and S. H. Losoya. "Prediction of Children's Empathy-Related Responding from Their Effortful Control and Parent's Expressivity." *Developmental Psychology* 40, no. 6 (2004): 911–926.

Vernon, D. T. A., and R. L. Blake. "Does Problem-Based Learning Work? A Meta-Analysis of Evaluative Research." *Academic Medicine* 68 (1993): 550–563.

Vygotsky, L. S. *Thought and Language,* trans. by A. Kozulin. Cambridge, MA: MIT Press, 1986.

Weinberger, D. R., B. Elvevåg, and J. Giedd. *The Adolescent Brain: A Work in Progress.* The National Campaign to Prevent Teen Pregnancy, 2005.

Wells, A. *Cognitive Therapy of Anxiety Disorders: A Practice Manual and Conceptual Guide.* Chichester, England: Wiley and Sons, 1997.

Werdmann, A. M. *Words and Feelings: Children's Vocabulary of Selected Emotions.* Dissertation thesis. ERIC, ED 132612.

Winnicott, D. W. *Collected Papers.* London: Tavistock Publications, 1958.

Wood, D. *How Children Think and Learn.* 2nd ed. Oxford: Blackwell, 1998.

Wood, D. J., J. Bruner, and G. Ross. "The Role of Tutoring in Problem Solving." *Journal of Child Psychology and Psychiatry* 17, no. 2 (1976): 89–100.

Topic Index

Index of Behaviors

angry outbursts, 20, 51-52, 138, 182
bossiness, 87-89
car accident, fear of, 155-157
class clown, 202
clowns, reaction to, 68-69
conflicting feelings, experiencing, 45-47
connecting thoughts and feelings, 77, 79
copying homework, 190
death of loved one, fear of, 155-157
delayed gratification in preschoolers, 28
divorce, children's fear of, 151-154
feelings, reading by infants, 31-32
groups, behavior in, 197
imaginary safe place, creating, 164
lateness for school, 218-220
mood swings, 129
moving to new home, 142
phobias, overcoming, 149-150
refusal to go to school, 89-90
school versus home behavior, 26
shy children, 183
spoiled children, 209-211
sports team selection, 104, 107
teasing, 193
toddler tantrums, calming, 35-36, 38

Index of Techniques

"bill of rights" technique (assertive
communication), 188, 190
"broken record" technique
(assertive communication),
190-192

conditioning techniques. *See* parenting,
behaviorist thinking in
diaphragmatic breathing technique,
158, 160
"downward arrow" technique, 89-90
"fogging" technique (assertive
communication), 192-194
graded exposure technique (overcoming
fears), 149-150
muscle relaxation technique,
160-161, 163
necessary conditions technique
(overcoming fears), 155-157
relaxation techniques. *See* muscle
relaxation technique; visualization
scaffolding technique, 114-115
self-soothing techniques, 158-163, 179.
See also visualization
sucking on candy (self-soothing
technique), 179
traffic light technique (anger
management), 177, 179-180
visualization, 163-166
for anger management, 178
guided visualization, 212-213, 215
hourglass image, 167
light image, 167-168
mental rehearsal of events, 168
in overriding negative thinking, 86
safe place, creating, 164-166
worst-case scenario technique
(overcoming fears), 151-154

Index

A

actions, matching with words, 35-36, 38.
   See also self-control
ADHD (Attention Deficit Hyperactivity
   Disorder), 170
adjourning stage (group
   development), 204
adolescence, brain development
   during, 24
aggressiveness. *See* anger
Allen, Woody, 127
amygdala, 23, 128
anger
   assertive communication versus, 184
   exaggerated language of, 182-183
   managing with traffic light technique,
      177, 179-180
   protective function of, 174-175
   situational causes of, 174-175
   thought habits of angry people,
      180-181
   warning signs of, 175, 177
anterior insula, 34
antidote thought, replacing negative
   thinking with, 94-96
anxiety. *See also* stress
   determining thoughts behind, 89-90
   discussing with children, 132
   in group behavior, 197
   overcoming
      graded exposure technique,
      149-150

necessary conditions technique,
   155-157
worst-case scenario technique,
   151-154
   as spectrum disorder, 102-103
   symptoms of, 129
assertive communication, 183-184,
   186-188
   anger versus, 184
   "bill of rights" technique, 188, 190
   body language, 186
   "broken record" technique, 190-192
   "fogging" technique, 192-194
   negotiation skills, 194, 196
   verbal skills, 184, 186
assessment tests, as cause of stress, 136
assumptions, challenging, 231-232
Attention Deficit Hyperactivity Disorder
   (ADHD), 170
attitudes for problem-solving, 226
   challenge assumptions, 231-232
   collaboration, 230
   learning from mistakes, 227-228
   perseverance, 228-229

B

bad behavior. *See also* behavior
   biological basis for, 22-23, 25
   in depressed children, 99
   as lack of mental energy, 25-26, 28
   as loss of self-control, 17, 19-21
   spoiled child example, 209-211
bashful children. *See* shy children
Baumeister, Ron, 27

In an increasingly competitive world, it is quality
of thinking that gives an edge—an idea that opens new
doors, a technique that solves a problem, or an insight
that simply helps make sense of it all.

We work with leading authors in the various arenas
of business and finance to bring cutting-edge thinking
and best-learning practices to a global market.

It is our goal to create world-class print publications
and electronic products that give readers
knowledge and understanding that can then be
applied, whether studying or at work.

To find out more about our business
products, you can visit us at www.ftpress.com.